20 MINUTE COOKBOOK

20 *MINUTE* COOKBOOK

STEVEN WHEELER

Photography by James Duncan

LORENZ BOOKS

This paperback edition published in 1998 by Lorenz Books
27 West 20th Street, New York, NY 10011

LORENZ BOOKS are available for bulk purchase for sales promotion and for
premium use. For details, write or call the sales director,
Lorenz Books, 27 West 20th Street, New York, NY 10011;
(800) 354-9657

© Anness Publishing Limited 1995

Lorenz Books is an imprint of
Anness Publishing Limited

ISBN 1 85967 696 0

A CIP catalogue record for this book
is available from the British Library

Publisher: Joanna Lorenz
Series Editor: Lindsay Porter
Designer: Peter Laws
Photographer: James Duncan
Stylist: Madeleine Brehaut

Printed and bound in Hong Kong

1 3 5 7 9 10 8 6 4 2

CONTENTS

INTRODUCTION

With only 20 minutes on the clock, and as much energy as anyone can have at the end of a busy day, we would all like to put good food on the table with minimum fuss. Every day we wonder what miracles we can perform with the usual ingredients. Rice, pasta and potatoes, chicken, ground beef and pork, all continue to call for fresh inspiration. Here are 50 recipes that promise to put renewed vigor and interest back into your everyday cooking.

Recipes divide into five chapters: starters, which could also be served as light meals, fish, meat and vegetarian dishes, and desserts. Ideas are based on the use of produce that is full of color, freshness and above all flavor. These qualities are essential to all cooking, but especially food that is prepared quickly.

Good cooking is about getting the maximum flavor from the main ingredients used. A piece of pork is good cooked plainly with simple seasoning, but throw in a few fresh sliced peaches and some soft green peppercorns and all three components will taste better and brighter. This sort of cooking is fast, intelligent and worthwhile, and is ideal for the mid-week rush. When you have a little more time to be with family and friends, a starter and/or dessert may be in order.

When one dish follows another, it is important for our comfort and digestion that they are well suited. A creamy soup does not, for instance, sit well with a rich main course. If you have the time to cook more than one course, turn to the carefully planned menus set out on pages 16–23. Preparation and cooking times vary for these menus, and some cooks will be quicker off the mark than others, but once you are familiar with a recipe, the timing will seem reasonable.

20 Minutes to Spare

Getting your act together enough to put a decent meal on the table day after day can take some doing. For many, cooking will always be a chore, while others will rise to the challenge and win. This section looks at ways to plan, shop and cook with as little effort as possible.

A lot of unnecessary running around can be prevented by sitting down with pencil and paper and drawing up a plan of action. Too often, ideas get the green light before realizing how much time and effort are needed to produce them. The first question to ask yourself is 'How much time and energy do I have?' Be realistic – a lot of cooks come unstuck when they take on more than they can handle. Be kind to yourself and choose something you can cope with. You'll not only enjoy preparing the meal, you might even be composed enough to sit down and enjoy it.

Cooking becomes a pleasure when we can recognize and choose the finest ingredients to work with. There is also a freedom to be had knowing which ingredients serve only to clutter our cupboards and refrigerators. Being able to see clearly what is good at a glance is one of the secrets of trouble-free cooking. Every item that we shop for has a value associated with price, flavor and convenience. If price exceeds flavor, reconsider. If flavor is lost for the sake of convenience – powdered mashed potato, for instance – you should think again. The cook's ultimatum should be flavor and convenience at the right price.

Shopping with a nose for flavor and freshness is the best way to fight through the consumer jungle and arrive home with quality produce. Choose well and give your cooking the head start that it deserves.

The following pages show what you might find in the cupboard of a flavor-conscious cook. Sweet and savory ingredients are best kept separate, apart from those that double up, such as flour, cornstarch, sugar and eggs. Ingredients that are used frequently, such as onions, garlic, oil, wine and fruit, make an attractive and convenient display kept on the work surface. All ingredients, whether in the cupboard or not, should be used up and replaced on a regular basis. Ground spices lose their punch after around eight months, so it makes sense to replace them with fresh. Nuts also lose their freshness and can taste rancid if kept past their sell-by date. With a well-stocked cupboard of basics in peak condition, the

idea of producing a tasty meal in 20 minutes needn't present quite so many problems.

Before starting, ask yourself three questions: How much time and energy do I have? What ingredients do I have in the refrigerator? What is the quickest way I can turn time, energy and ingredients into a satisfying meal? Develop a strategy on paper that shows exactly what you are cooking, what shopping you need and where you have to go to get it. Do your shopping in one stop and try to write your list in accordance with the layout of the store. Backtracking for the last few items on your list is no one's idea of fun.

When even the simplest meals are properly thought out,

three-quarters of the work is done. From your list you know exactly what you are cooking, what shopping you need, where to get it and what you are going to do with the ingredients when you start to get to work in the kitchen.

It's always worth taking a few minutes to read a recipe through before you start. This should enable you to have all the necessary equipment to hand from the outset. It has to be said that some cooks are more organized in their kitchens than others. Some cooks clean and tidy up with near-surgical precision, while others thrive in varying degrees of chaos. Cooking quickly

depends on: a) knowing what you are doing, and b) being able to put your hands on what you need as you go. Most cooks work best of all in a relatively creative mess where somehow everything comes together in the end. Whatever conditions you are comfortable with, make sure they are 'just so' before you begin cooking.

Kitchen Cupboard Staples

The following ingredients are shown left to right from the top shelf.

Polenta
Italian cornmeal. Serve with Gorgonzola cheese and salad.

Flour
All-purpose and self-rising flour are used for making white sauces and pancakes.

Lentils
Red lentils soften quickly for simple soups and sauces.

Couscous
Cracked wheat for tabbouleh-style salads.

Sesame seeds
Nutty and rich when toasted. Sprinkle over an omelette.

Spices
Cumin, coriander, fennel seed, cardamom and peppercorns are best when freshly ground.

Pasta
Use best quality fine vermicelli for soups, and spaghetti and other pasta shapes with sauces.

Wild mushrooms
Deeply flavored dried porcini and morels revive in hot water.

Fresh herbs
Parsley, thyme, garlic and rosemary add instant flavor.

Long-grain and risotto rice
These take a little longer to cook but are full of flavor.

Almonds
These provide a rich flavor in sauces and salsas.

Buckwheat
Robustly flavored grain. Cook with couscous.

Garlic in oil
Garlic cloves keep their flavor in olive oil (see page 14).

Tarragon in vinegar
Keep fresh tarragon in wine vinegar for year-round flavor.

Pine nuts
The intensely rich fruit of the pine cone. A great asset to vegetarian dishes.

Stock cubes
Good quality stock cubes are indispensable. Buy the additive-free type if you can.

Cornstarch
This is used for thickening sauces and gravies.

Capers
The fairly sharp taste of capers makes an ideal accompaniment to meat dishes.

Mustard
A piquant addition to meats and savory sauces.

Green peppercorns
Soft berries with an assertive heat. Delicious with pork.

Pesto sauce
Made from basil, garlic, pine nuts, cheese and olive oil. Use for speedy pasta dishes.

Pasta sauce
Make your own from a can of tomatoes (see page 15). Serve with an Italian hard cheese.

Canned vegetables
Young peas and beans in brine are easy to serve with grilled meat and fish.

Citrus fruits
Bright oranges, lemons and limes offer fresh fruit flavors to savory cooking.

Onions
Onions, like garlic and ginger root, add delicious flavor to a variety of dishes.

Wine
Sober judgment allows a measure of wine, as and when it pleases the cook!

Oils
Keep olive oil for flavor, and a variety such as groundnut for neutral taste.

Vinegar
Use a good white wine vinegar. Balsamic vinegar should be used only sparingly.

Olives and pickled peppers
Good olives and pickled peppers will provide a taste of the sun in the winter.

Eggs
Fast-food convenience in a shell. Properly fed hens lay the best and tastiest eggs.

Dessert Kitchen Cupboard Staples

The following ingredients are shown left to right from the center shelf.

Flour
Plain and self-rising flour can be used for fast sponges, tarts and easy pancakes.

Superfine sugar
This is a free-flow, fast-mix, easy-blend sugar suited to all good cakes and baked goods.

Confectioners' sugar
This is powder-fine for easy icing and dusting. Sift before using to remove any lumps.

Meringues
Store-bought meringues kept in an airtight jar can be used for impromptu desserts.

Chocolate sauce
Make your own (see page 15). Delicious with ice cream, sprinkled with toasted nuts.

Cocoa powder
Use sugarless cocoa powder in drinks and desserts for a rich chocolate taste.

Chocolate
Buy the best quality chocolate you can afford and store it at room temperature, never in the refrigerator.

Cornstarch
Use this combined half-and-half with flour for fine textured cakes and sponges.

Citrus fruits
Oranges, lemons and limes offer zestful flavor. Heavy fruits offer the juiciest squeeze.

Cherries
Enjoy these fresh in season, as they have a poor flavor when cooked. Choose sour, or buy canned for cooking.

Melon
Fill your kitchen with the scent of a ripe melon. Serve cold with red berry fruit when in season.

Bananas
Bananas are deliciously sweet when speckled brown.

Pineapple
Pineapples are ripe when the skin smells sweet.

Strawberries
Traditionally served with sugar and cream, but also ideal for use in hot and cold desserts, cakes and tarts.

Pears
Partner pears with Parmesan, Pecorino, Gorgonzola or Roquefort cheeses.

Apples
Red, green and russet skins conceal a host of flavor. All these apples make a juicy and crisp addition to quick desserts.

Peaches
Remove the skins from sun-ripened peaches by plunging in boiling water.

Passionfruit
The sour, scented juice of this fruit is delicious when combined with strawberries and raspberries.

Grapes
There are innumerable varieties of grapes available, and they can be red, green or seedless. Muscat grapes offer the best flavor and sweetness.

Finger wafers
These and other ice cream accessories are a must for spur-of-the-moment desserts.

Brown sugar
Less refined than white, brown sugars are rich in molasses. Dark sugars are stronger in taste.

Flaked almonds
Uninteresting raw, a temptation when toasted. Scatter over ice cream, chocolate and summer fruit for the finishing touch.

Ground almonds
Essential for moist cakes and sponges; substitute half flour with ground almonds in any baking recipe.

Preserved fruit
Use canned or bottled apricots and raspberries for easy convenience in desserts.

Eggs
Store and use eggs at room temperature.

Salad Dressing Baste

A good salad dressing can double up as an effective baste for the broiler and barbecue. This dressing is delicious with white meats as well as fish.

Makes 7 tbsp

INGREDIENTS
6 tbsp olive oil
1 tbsp white wine vinegar
1 tsp French mustard
½ garlic clove, crushed
¼ tsp sugar

1 Pour the oil and vinegar into a screw-topped jar.

2 Add the mustard, garlic and sugar.

3 Shake well, and use as a dressing or marinade for salad, meat and fish.

Garlic Oil

To capture the freshness of garlic, keep crushed cloves in olive oil and use in dressings, sauces and for cooking.

Makes ½ cup

INGREDIENTS
6–8 garlic cloves
½ cup olive oil

1 Trim the root end from 6–8 cloves of garlic. Tap each clove sharply under the side of a large knife, banging with a fist until the clove splits and the skin loosens. Discard the skin.

2 Use the back of a heavy knife, near the handle, to crush the garlic. Hold firmly with the end of the blade resting on the chopping board, secure the clove with your thumb and forefinger, then crush with a chopping motion.

3 Transfer the crushed garlic into a screw-topped jar, cover with olive oil and store at room temperature. The oil will keep for up to two weeks.

COOK'S TIP

Garlic and other substances are not preserved in oil, and there is concern that bacteria may form if kept too long. Do not keep the oil longer than two weeks. If kept in the refrigerator the oil may solidify, but can be used if left to soften at room temperature.

Pasta Sauce

Keep this easy sauce in mind when you want a tomato topping for pasta.

Makes 3²/₃ cups

INGREDIENTS
2 × 14 oz cans chopped tomatoes
4 tbsp olive oil
2 garlic cloves, crushed
2 tsp fresh or dried thyme
2 tsp anchovy paste (optional)
½ tsp black olive paste (optional)
½ tsp freshly ground black pepper

2 Heat the oil and garlic in a saucepan and add the thyme, sieved tomatoes, anchovy essence and olive paste, if using. Simmer for 5 minutes, then season to taste with black pepper. Liquidize in a blender if you like a smooth sauce.

1 Empty the tomatoes into a nylon sieve set over a bowl. The juices will run clear after a short time. Allow the tomatoes to thicken for 10 minutes.

3 If you are not using the sauce immediately, spoon into a preserving jar. This sauce will keep refrigerated for up to seven days.

Chocolate Sauce

Every cook should have a jar of chocolate sauce to hand for last minute dessert making. Serve hot or cold over ice cream, steamed puddings and pastries.

Makes 1 cup

INGREDIENTS
²/₃ cup light cream
1 tbsp superfine sugar
5 oz best quality plain chocolate, broken
2 tbsp dark rum or whisky (optional)

1 Rinse out a small saucepan with cold water to prevent the sauce from sticking. Bring the cream and sugar to a boil.

2 Remove from the heat, add the chocolate and stir until melted. Stir in the alcohol, if using.

3 Pour the chocolate sauce into a closed jar. When cool, refrigerate for up to ten days. Reheat by standing the jar in a saucepan of simmering water, or microwave on high power (100%) for 2 minutes and stir.

Menu Planner

All of the recipes in this book can be prepared individually in 20 minutes or less. However, they can all be combined with other dishes to provide a two- or three-course meal when you have a little more time available. Below and on the following pages are some suggested menus, explaining how to coordinate the preparation and cooking times required, so that you can prepare two or more courses simultaneously. To follow the menus, work across each row, from left to right, and then down the chart to the end.

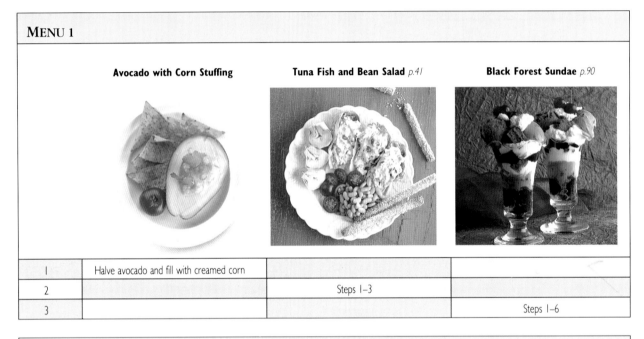

MENU 1			
	Avocado with Corn Stuffing	**Tuna Fish and Bean Salad** *p.41*	**Black Forest Sundae** *p.90*
1	Halve avocado and fill with creamed corn		
2		Steps 1–3	
3			Steps 1–6

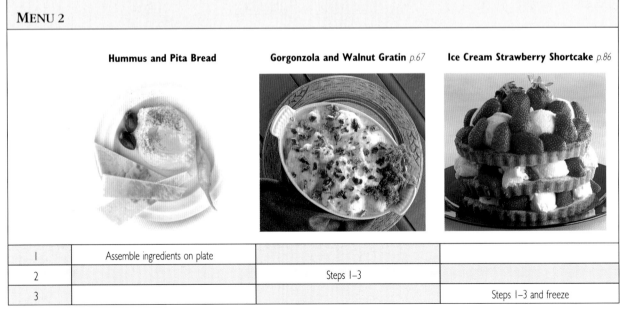

MENU 2			
	Hummus and Pita Bread	**Gorgonzola and Walnut Gratin** *p.67*	**Ice Cream Strawberry Shortcake** *p.86*
1	Assemble ingredients on plate		
2		Steps 1–3	
3			Steps 1–3 and freeze

MENU 3

	Buckwheat Couscous p.35	Fillets of Pink Trout p.38	Strawberries and Cream
1	Steps 1–2		
2		Steps 1–5	
3			Hull strawberries, assemble with cream
4	Step 3		
5		Step 6	

MENU 4

	Prosciutto, Sausage and Olives	Grilled Snapper p.46	Raspberry Puffs p.82
1		Steps 1–2	
2	Assemble ingredients with artichoke hearts		
3			Steps 1–4
4		Steps 4–6	
5			Steps 5–6

MENU 5

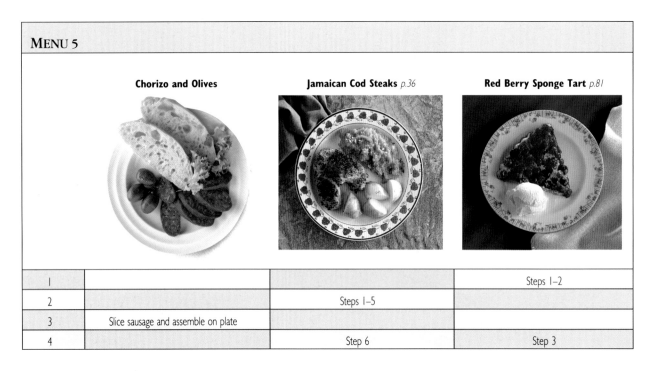

Chorizo and Olives   **Jamaican Cod Steaks** *p.36*   **Red Berry Sponge Tart** *p.81*

1			Steps 1–2
2		Steps 1–5	
3	Slice sausage and assemble on plate		
4		Step 6	Step 3

MENU 6

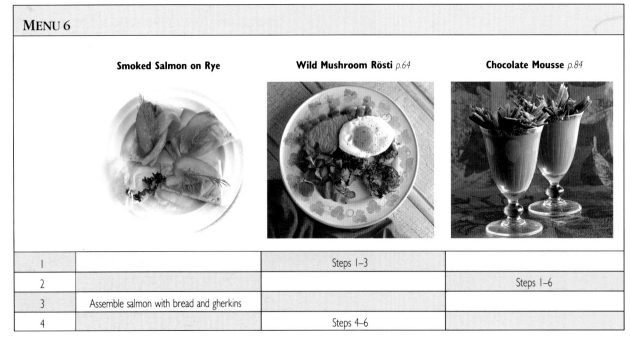

Smoked Salmon on Rye   **Wild Mushroom Rösti** *p.64*   **Chocolate Mousse** *p.84*

1		Steps 1–3	
2			Steps 1–6
3	Assemble salmon with bread and gherkins		
4		Steps 4–6	

MENU 7

Beet and Lima Bean Soup *p.28* **Mushroom Macaroni and Cheese** *p.73* **Pineapple, Strawberries and Sorbet**

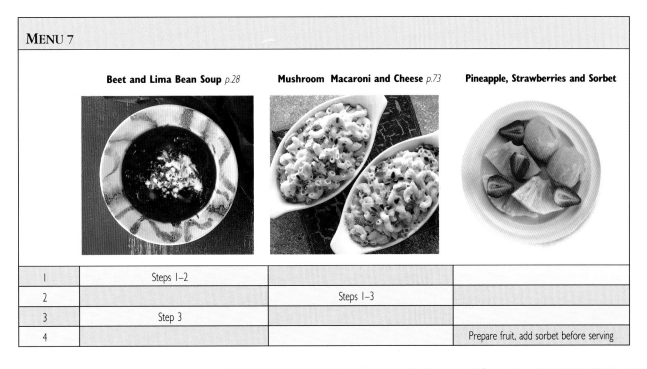

	Beet and Lima Bean Soup	Mushroom Macaroni and Cheese	Pineapple, Strawberries and Sorbet
1	Steps 1–2		
2		Steps 1–3	
3	Step 3		
4			Prepare fruit, add sorbet before serving

MENU 8

Baby Carrot and Fennel Soup *p.29* **Sausage Popovers** *p.62* **Melon and Berries**

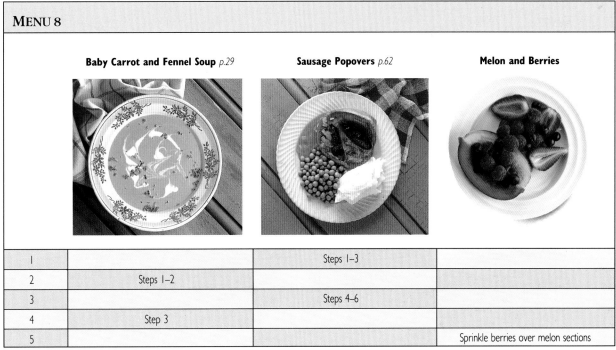

	Baby Carrot and Fennel Soup	Sausage Popovers	Melon and Berries
1		Steps 1–3	
2	Steps 1–2		
3		Steps 4–6	
4	Step 3		
5			Sprinkle berries over melon sections

MENU 9

	Melon and Prosciutto	Dover Sole in a Parsley Jacket *p.44*	Apples in Rose Pouchong Syrup *p.94*

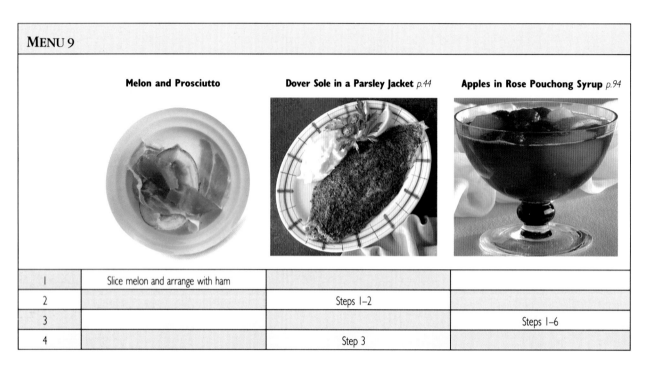

1	Slice melon and arrange with ham		
2		Steps 1–2	
3			Steps 1–6
4		Step 3	

MENU 10

	Stuffed Garlic Mushrooms *p.30*	Spinach and Ricotta Shells *p.76*	Peaches and Yogurt

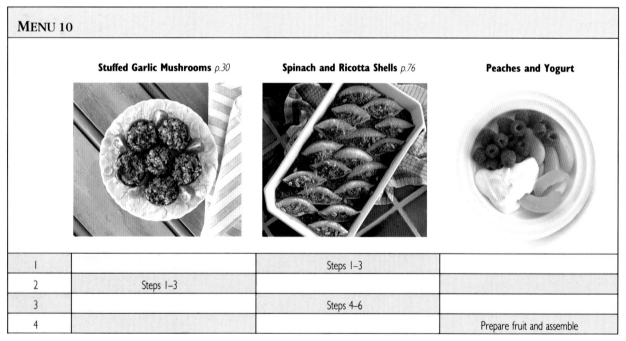

1		Steps 1–3	
2	Steps 1–3		
3		Steps 4–6	
4			Prepare fruit and assemble

MENU 11

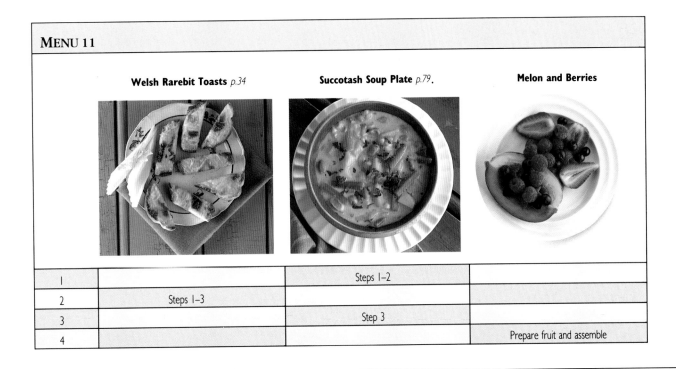

Welsh Rarebit Toasts *p.34* **Succotash Soup Plate** *p.79.* **Melon and Berries**

1		Steps 1–2	
2	Steps 1–3		
3		Step 3	
4			Prepare fruit and assemble

MENU 12

Crab and Egg Noodle Broth *p.26* **Indonesian Pork and Peanut Saté** *p.59* **Pineapple, Strawberries and Sorbet**

1			Prepare fruit, add sorbet before serving
2		Steps 1–2	
3	Steps 1–6		
4		Step 3	

MENU 13

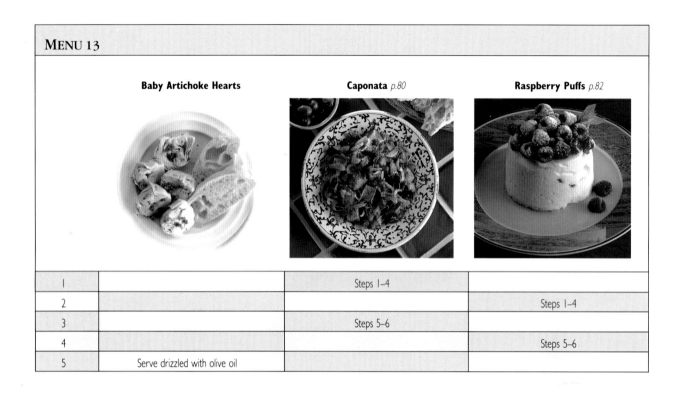

Baby Artichoke Hearts **Caponata** *p.80* **Raspberry Puffs** *p.82*

	Baby Artichoke Hearts	Caponata	Raspberry Puffs
1		Steps 1–4	
2			Steps 1–4
3		Steps 5–6	
4			Steps 5–6
5	Serve drizzled with olive oil		

MENU 14

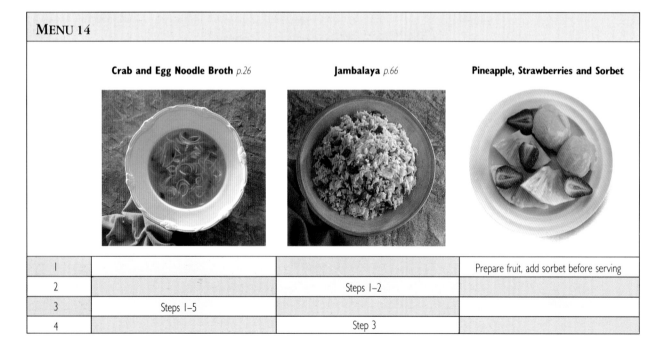

Crab and Egg Noodle Broth *p.26* **Jambalaya** *p.66* **Pineapple, Strawberries and Sorbet**

	Crab and Egg Noodle Broth	Jambalaya	Pineapple, Strawberries and Sorbet
1			Prepare fruit, add sorbet before serving
2		Steps 1–2	
3	Steps 1–5		
4		Step 3	

MENU 15

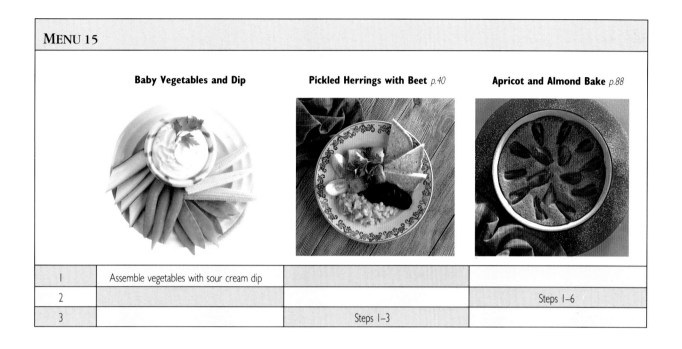

Baby Vegetables and Dip **Pickled Herrings with Beet** *p.40* **Apricot and Almond Bake** *p.88*

	Baby Vegetables and Dip	Pickled Herrings with Beet	Apricot and Almond Bake
1	Assemble vegetables with sour cream dip		
2			Steps 1–6
3		Steps 1–3	

MENU 16

Stuffed Garlic Mushrooms *p.30* **Spanish Omelet** *p.70* **Fresh Figs, Chocolate and Liqueur**

	Stuffed Garlic Mushrooms	Spanish Omelet	Fresh Figs, Chocolate and Liqueur
1	Steps 1–3		
2		Steps 1–6	
3			Fill figs with chocolate and drizzle with liqueur

Fresh Pea and Ham Soup

Frozen peas provide flavor, freshness and color in this delicious winter soup, which is filling enough to make a light main course or a starter.

Serves 4

INGREDIENTS
4 oz small pasta shapes
2 tbsp vegetable oil
1 small bunch scallions, chopped
3 cups frozen peas
5 cups chicken stock
8 oz raw unsmoked ham
   or bacon
4 tbsp heavy cream
salt and freshly ground black pepper
warm crusty bread, to serve

PREPARATION TIME

10 minutes

COOKING TIME

10 minutes

ham

pasta

cream

peas

scallions

1 Bring a large saucepan of salted water to a boil. Toss in the pasta and cook according to the instructions on the package. Drain, cover with cold water and set aside until required.

2 Heat the vegetable oil in a large heavy saucepan and cook the scallions until soft. Add the peas and stock, then simmer for 10 minutes.

3 Liquidize the soup in a blender and return to the saucepan. Cut the ham or bacon into short fingers and add it together with the pasta to the saucepan. Simmer for 2–3 minutes and season to taste. Stir in the cream and serve with the warm crusty bread.

VARIATION

Any pasta shapes can be used for this soup, although hoops or shells seem to work best of all.

French Onion Soup

In the time it takes to soften a few onions and brown some cheese on toast, this delicious soup appears on the table steaming hot and ready to eat. It makes a substantial starter or lunch dish.

Serves 4

INGREDIENTS
2 tbsp vegetable oil
3 medium onions, sliced
3¾ cups beef stock
4 slices French bread
butter, for spreading
1 cup grated Gruyère, Beaufort or
  Emmenthal cheese

PREPARATION TIME
10 minutes

COOKING TIME
10 minutes

onions

cheese

French bread

1 Heat the vegetable oil in a large frying pan and brown the onions over a steady heat, taking care they do not burn.

2 Transfer the browned onions to a large saucepan, cover with beef stock and simmer for 10 minutes.

3 Preheat the broiler to a moderate temperature and toast the French bread on both sides. Spread one side with butter and top with grated cheese. Ladle the soup into four flameproof dishes, float the cheesy crusts on top and grill until crispy and brown.

COOK'S TIP
The flavor and richness of French onion soup will improve if the soup is kept chilled in the refrigerator for three to four days.

Crab and Egg Noodle Broth

This delicious broth is an ideal solution when you are hungry and time is short, and you need something fast, nutritious and filling.

Serves 4

INGREDIENTS

3 oz fine egg noodles
2 tbsp unsalted butter
1 small bunch scallions, chopped
1 celery stick, sliced
1 medium carrot, peeled and cut
  into sticks
5 cups chicken stock
4 tbsp dry sherry
4 oz white crab meat, fresh
  or frozen
pinch of celery salt
pinch of cayenne pepper
2 tsp lemon juice
1 small bunch cilantro or flat-leaf
  parsley, to garnish

PREPARATION AND COOKING TIME

20 minutes

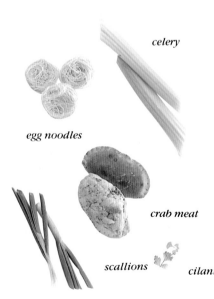

celery

egg noodles

crab meat

scallions   *cilantro*

Fresh or frozen crab meat has the best flavor. Avoid canned crab, as this tastes rather bland.

1 Bring a large saucepan of salted water to a boil. Toss in the egg noodles and cook according to the instructions on the package. Cool under cold running water and leave immersed in water until required.

2 Heat the butter in another large pan, add the scallions, celery and carrot, cover and soften the vegetables over a gentle heat for 3–4 minutes.

3 Add the chicken stock and sherry, bring to a boil and simmer for a further 5 minutes.

4 Flake the crab meat between your fingers onto a plate and remove any stray pieces of shell.

5 Drain the noodles and add to the broth together with the crab meat. Season to taste with celery salt and cayenne pepper, and sharpen with the lemon juice. Return to a simmer.

6 Ladle the broth into shallow soup plates, scatter with roughly chopped cilantro or parsley and serve.

Speedy Beet and Lima Bean Soup

This soup is a simplified version of borscht, and is prepared in a fraction of the time. Serve with a spoonful of sour cream and a scattering of chopped fresh parsley.

Serves 4

INGREDIENTS

2 tbsp vegetable oil
1 medium onion, halved and sliced
1 tsp caraway seeds
finely grated zest of ½ orange
9 oz cooked beets, grated
5 cups fresh or canned beef stock
   or rassol
1 × 14 oz can lima beans, drained
1 tbsp wine vinegar
4 tbsp sour cream
4 tbsp chopped fresh parsley,
   to garnish

PREPARATION AND COOKING TIME

20 minutes

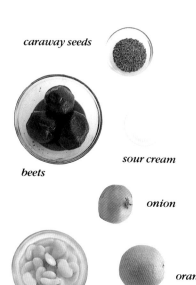

caraway seeds

sour cream

beets

onion

orange

beans

1 Heat the oil in a large saucepan and cook the onion, caraway seeds and orange zest until soft but not colored.

2 Add the beets, stock, lima beans and vinegar and simmer for a further 10 minutes.

COOK'S TIP

Rassol is a beet broth used for its strong color and flavor. You are most likely to find it in Kosher food stores.

3 Divide the soup between four bowls, add a spoonful of sour cream to each and scatter with chopped fresh parsley.

Baby Carrot and Fennel Soup

Sweet tender carrots find their moment of glory in this delicately spiced soup. Fennel provides an anise flavor without overpowering the carrots.

Serves 4

INGREDIENTS
4 tbsp butter
1 small bunch scallions, chopped
5 oz fennel bulb, chopped
1 celery stalk, chopped
1 lb baby carrots, grated
½ tsp ground cumin
5 oz new potatoes, peeled and diced
5 cups fresh or canned chicken or
    vegetable stock
4 tbsp heavy cream
salt and freshly ground black pepper
4 tbsp chopped fresh parsley,
    to garnish

PREPARATION TIME

5 minutes

COOKING TIME

15 minutes

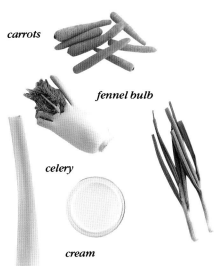

carrots

fennel bulb

celery

cream

scallions

1 Melt the butter in a large saucepan and add the scallions, fennel, celery, carrots and cumin. Cover and cook for 5 minutes until soft.

2 Add the potatoes and stock, and simmer for a further 10 minutes.

3 Liquidize the mixture in the pan with a hand-held mixer. Stir in the cream and season to taste. Serve in individual bowls and garnish with chopped fresh parsley.

COOK'S TIP

For convenience, you can freeze the soup in portions before adding the cream, seasoning and parsley.

Stuffed Garlic Mushrooms with a Parsley Crust

These garlic mushrooms are perfect for dinner parties, or you could serve them in larger portions as a light supper dish with a green salad. Try them stuffed with a healthy dose of freshly chopped parsley.

Serves 4

INGREDIENTS

12 oz large field mushrooms, stems removed
3 garlic cloves, crushed
¾ cup butter, softened
3 cups finely crumbled fresh white breadcrumbs
1 cup fresh parsley, chopped
1 egg, beaten
salt and cayenne pepper
8 cherry tomatoes, to garnish

PREPARATION TIME

10 minutes

COOKING TIME

10 minutes

parsley

butter   *egg*

garlic

mushrooms

breadcrumbs

1 Preheat the oven to 375°F. Arrange the mushrooms cup side uppermost on a baking tray. Mix together the crushed garlic and butter in a small bowl and divide ½ cup of the butter between the mushrooms.

2 Heat the remaining butter in a frying pan and lightly fry the breadcrumbs until golden brown. Place the chopped parsley in a bowl, add the breadcrumbs, season to taste and mix well.

3 Stir in the egg and use the mixture to fill the mushroom caps. Bake for 10–15 minutes until the topping has browned and the mushrooms have softened. Garnish with quartered tomatoes.

COOK'S TIP

If you are planning ahead, stuffed mushrooms can be prepared up to 12 hours in advance and kept in the fridge before baking.

Smoked Trout and Horseradish Salad

Salads are the easy answer to fast, healthy eating. When lettuce is sweet and crisp, partner it with fillets of smoked trout, warm new potatoes and a creamy horseradish dressing.

Serves 4

INGREDIENTS
1½ lb new potatoes
4 smoked trout fillets
4 oz mixed lettuce leaves
4 slices dark rye bread, cut into
    fingers
salt and freshly ground black pepper

FOR THE DRESSING
4 tbsp creamed horseradish
4 tbsp groundnut oil
1 tbsp white wine vinegar
2 tsp caraway seeds

PREPARATION AND COOKING TIME

20 minutes

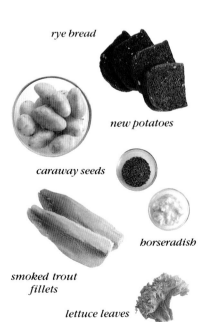

rye bread

new potatoes

caraway seeds

horseradish

smoked trout fillets

lettuce leaves

1 Bring the potatoes to a boil in a saucepan of salted water and simmer for 20 minutes. Remove the skin from the trout, and lift the flesh from the bone.

2 To make the dressing, place all the ingredients in a screw-topped jar and shake vigorously. Season the lettuce leaves and moisten them with the prepared dressing. Distribute between four plates.

3 Flake the trout fillets and halve the potatoes. Scatter them together with the rye fingers over the salad leaves and toss to mix. Season to taste and serve.

COOK'S TIP

To save time washing lettuce leaves, buy them ready-prepared from your supermarket. It is better to season the leaves rather than the dressing when making a salad.

Smoked Salmon Crêpes with Pesto and Pine Nuts

These simple crêpes take no more than 10–15 minutes to prepare and are perfect for a special occasion. Smoked salmon is delicious with fresh basil and combines well with toasted pine nuts and a spoonful of crème fraîche or heavy cream.

Makes 12–16

INGREDIENTS
½ cup milk
1 cup self-rising flour
1 egg
2 tbsp pesto sauce
vegetable oil, for frying
scant 1 cup crème fraîche or heavy cream
3 oz smoked salmon
1 tbsp pine nuts, toasted
salt and freshly ground black pepper
12–16 fresh basil sprigs, to garnish

PREPARATION TIME
10 minutes

COOKING TIME
10 minutes

basil

pine nuts

crème fraîche

flour

pesto sauce

smoked salmon

1 Pour half of the milk into a mixing bowl. Add the flour, egg, pesto sauce and seasoning and mix to a smooth batter.

2 Add the remainder of the milk and stir until evenly blended.

3 Heat the vegetable oil in a large frying pan. Spoon the crêpe mixture into the heated oil in small heaps. Allow about 30 seconds for the crêpes to cook, then turn and cook briefly on the other side. Continue cooking the crêpes in batches until all the batter is used up.

4 Arrange the crêpes on a serving plate and top each one with a spoonful of crème fraîche or heavy cream.

5 Cut the salmon into 1 cm/½ in strips and place on top of each crêpe.

COOK'S TIP
If not serving immediately, cover the crêpes with a dish towel and keep warm in an oven preheated to 275°F.

6 Scatter each crêpe with pine nuts and garnish with a sprig of fresh basil.

Welsh Rarebit Toasts

Welsh Rarebit is the gourmet's answer to cheese on toast. Serve as a tasty starter with drinks.

Serves 4

INGREDIENTS
scant 1 cup beer
4 tbsp flour
2 tsp mustard (powdered or
   ready-made)
½ tsp celery salt
pinch of cayenne pepper
1½ cups grated Cheddar
   cheese
6 thick slices white or whole wheat
   bread
3 celery stalks, to serve

PREPARATION TIME
15 minutes

COOKING TIME
5 minutes

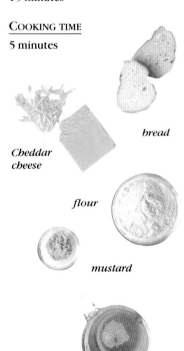

bread

Cheddar cheese

flour

mustard

beer

1 Measure ¼ cup of the beer into a mixing bowl and combine with the flour, mustard, celery salt and cayenne pepper. Mix well.

2 Bring the remaining beer to a boil in a heavy saucepan together with the cheese. Pour over the mixed ingredients and stir to blend evenly. Return to the saucepan and simmer gently, stirring continuously, to thicken.

3 Preheat a moderate broiler and toast the bread on both sides. Spread thickly with the mixture, then broil until golden brown and bubbly. Cut into fingers and serve with celery stalks.

COOK'S TIP
Welsh Rarebit mixture will keep in the refrigerator for up to a week and is perfect for a fast snack at any time of the day.

Buckwheat Couscous with Goat Cheese and Celery

Couscous is made from cracked, partially cooked wheat, which is dried and then reconstituted in water or stock. It tastes of very little by itself, but carries the flavor of other ingredients very well.

Serves 4

INGREDIENTS
1 egg
2 tbsp olive oil
1 small bunch scallions, chopped
2 celery stalks, sliced
1 cup couscous
½ cup buckwheat
3 tbsp chopped fresh parsley
finely grated zest of ½ lemon
¼ cup chopped walnuts, toasted
5 oz strongly flavored goat
   cheese
salt and freshly ground black pepper
Romaine lettuce leaves, to serve

PREPARATION TIME

5 minutes

COOKING TIME

15 minutes

buckwheat

celery

egg

goat cheese

parsley

walnuts

1 Boil the egg for 10 minutes, cool, peel and set aside. Heat the oil in a saucepan and add the scallions and celery. Cook for 2–3 minutes until soft.

2 Add the couscous and buckwheat and cover with 2½ cups of boiling salted water. Cover and return to a simmer. Remove from the heat and allow the couscous to soften and absorb the water for about 3 minutes. Transfer the mixture to a large bowl.

3 Grate the hard-boiled egg finely into a small bowl and add the chopped parsley, lemon zest and walnuts. Fold into the couscous, season, and crumble in the goat cheese. Mix well and then turn out into a shallow dish. Serve warm with a salad of Romaine lettuce.

VARIATION

Couscous is ideal as a filling for pita breads when accompanied with crisp salad leaves.

Jamaican Spiced Cod Steaks with Pumpkin Ragout

Spicy hot from Kingston town, this fast fish dish is guaranteed to appeal. The term 'ragout' is taken from the old French verb *ragouter*, which means to stimulate the appetite.

Serves 4

INGREDIENTS
finely grated zest of ½ orange
2 tbsp black peppercorns
1 tbsp allspice berries or Jamaican
   pepper
½ tsp salt
4 × 6 oz cod steaks
groundnut oil, for frying
new potatoes, to serve (optional)
3 tbsp chopped fresh parsley,
   to garnish

FOR THE RAGOUT
2 tbsp groundnut oil
1 medium onion, chopped
1 in fresh ginger root, peeled and
   grated
1 lb fresh pumpkin, peeled, deseeded
   and chopped
3–4 shakes of Tabasco sauce
2 tbsp soft brown sugar
1 tbsp vinegar

PREPARATION AND COOKING TIME

20 minutes

pumpkin

cod steaks

ginger

COOK'S TIP
This recipe can be adapted using any types of firm pink or white fish that is available, such as haddock, whiting, monkfish, halibut or tuna.

1 To make the ragout, heat the oil in a heavy saucepan and add the onion and ginger. Cover and cook, stirring, for 3–4 minutes until soft.

2 Add the chopped pumpkin, Tabasco sauce, brown sugar and vinegar, cover and cook over a low heat for 10–12 minutes until softened.

3 Combine the orange zest, peppercorns, allspice or Jamaican pepper and salt, then crush coarsely using a pestle and mortar. (Alternatively, coarsely grind the peppercorns in a pepper mill and combine with the zest and seasoning.)

4 Scatter the spice mixture over both sides of the fish and moisten with a sprinkling of oil.

5 Heat a large frying pan and fry the cod steaks for 12 minutes, turning once.

6 Serve the cod steaks with a spoonful of pumpkin ragout and new potatoes, if desired, and garnish the ragout with chopped fresh parsley.

Fillets of Pink Trout with Tarragon Cream Sauce

If you do not like the idea of cooking and serving trout on the bone, ask your fishmonger to fillet and skin the fish. Serve two fillets per person.

Serves 4

INGREDIENTS
2 tbsp butter
4 fresh trout, filleted and skinned
salt and freshly ground black pepper
new potatoes, to serve
wax beans, to serve

FOR THE CREAM SAUCE
2 large scallions, white part only, chopped
½ cucumber, peeled, deseeded and cut into short sticks
1 tsp cornstarch
⅔ cup light cream
¼ cup dry sherry
2 tbsp chopped fresh tarragon
1 tomato, chopped and deseeded

PREPARATION AND COOKING TIME
20 minutes

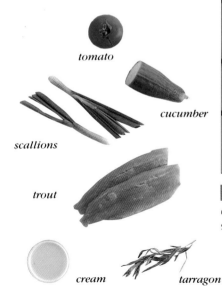

tomato

cucumber

scallions

trout

cream   *tarragon*

VARIATION
This recipe can also be made with salmon fillets and the dry sherry may be substituted with white wine.

1 Melt the butter in a large frying pan, season the fillets and cook for 6 minutes, turning once. Transfer to a plate, cover and keep warm.

2 To make the sauce, add the scallions and cucumber to the pan, and cook over a gentle heat, stirring occasionally, until soft but not colored.

3 Remove the pan from the heat and stir in the cornstarch.

4 Return to the heat and pour in the cream and sherry. Simmer to thicken, stirring continuously.

5 Add the chopped tarragon and tomato, and season to taste.

6 Spoon the sauce over the fillets and serve with buttered new potatoes and wax beans.

Pickled Herrings with Beet and Apple Relish

Soused or pickled herrings are delicious with cooked beets. Serve with buttered rye bread and a sweet and sour apple relish.

Serves 4

INGREDIENTS
2 eggs
8 pickled herrings
9 oz cooked baby beet
fresh flat-leaf parsley, to garnish
4 slices buttered rye bread, to serve
⅔ cup sour cream, to serve
  (optional)

FOR THE RELISH
2 tbsp vegetable oil
2 large apples, peeled, cored and
  finely chopped
1 medium onion, chopped
1 tbsp sugar
1 tbsp cider vinegar
1 tsp hot mustard
pinch of salt

PREPARATION TIME

15 minutes

COOKING TIME

5 minutes

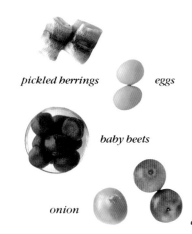

pickled herrings   *eggs*

baby beets

onion   *apples*

1 Bring a saucepan of water to a boil, gently lower in the eggs and cook for 10 minutes. Cool under running water and peel. Cut into quarters.

2 To make the relish, heat the oil in a saucepan and add the apple and onion. Cook over a gentle heat for 3–4 minutes without coloring. Add the sugar, vinegar and mustard, then season with salt.

COOK'S TIP

Choose full-flavored green or red apples for the best results.

3 Divide the herrings between four plates. Slice the beets and arrange to one side with the relish. Decorate with egg quarters and garnish with parsley. Serve with buttered rye bread, and a spoonful of sour cream if you wish.

Tuna Fish and Flageolet Bean Salad

Two cans of tuna fish form the basis of this delicious store cupboard salad.

Serves 4

INGREDIENTS
6 tbsp mayonnaise
1 tsp mustard
2 tbsp capers
3 tbsp chopped fresh parsley
pinch of celery salt
2 × 7 oz cans tuna fish in oil, drained
3 Bibb lettuces
1 × 14 oz can flageolet beans, drained
1 × 14 oz can baby artichoke hearts, halved
12 cherry tomatoes, halved
toasted sesame bread, to serve

PREPARATION TIME
15 minutes

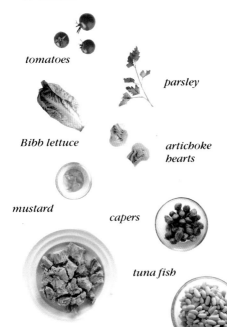

tomatoes

parsley

Bibb lettuce

artichoke hearts

mustard

capers

tuna fish

flageolet beans

1 Combine the mayonnaise, mustard, capers and parsley in a mixing bowl. Season to taste with celery salt. Flake the tuna into the dressing and toss gently.

2 Arrange the lettuce leaves on four plates, then spoon the tuna mixture onto the leaves.

3 Spoon the flageolet beans to one side, followed by the tomatoes and artichoke hearts. Serve with slices of toasted sesame bread.

VARIATION
Flageolet beans are taken from the under-developed pods of navy beans. They have a sweet creamy flavor and an attractive green color. If not available, use cannellini beans.

English Muffins with Sole, Spinach and Mushrooms

English muffins, frozen spinach and a few mushrooms form the beginning of this nourishing fish course. Any flatfish will do, although sole works best of all.

Serves 2

INGREDIENTS

½ cup butter, plus extra for
   buttering muffins
1 medium onion, chopped
4 oz cremini mushrooms,
   sliced
2 fresh thyme sprigs, chopped
10 oz frozen leaf spinach, thawed
3 lb sole or flounder to yield
   1½ lb skinned fillet
2 white English muffins, split
4 tbsp crème fraîche or heavy cream
salt and freshly ground black pepper

PREPARATION AND COOKING TIME

20 minutes

English muffins

spinach

crème fraîche

sole

thyme

onion

1 Heat 4 tbsp of the butter in a saucepan and add the onion. Cook over a gentle heat until soft but not colored.

2 Add the mushrooms and thyme, cover and cook for a further 2–3 minutes. Remove the lid and increase the heat to drive off excess moisture.

3 Using the back of a large spoon, press the thawed frozen spinach in a sieve to extract the moisture.

4 Heat a further 2 tbsp butter in a saucepan, add the spinach, heat through and season to taste.

5 Melt the remaining butter in a large frying pan, season the fillets and, with skin side uppermost, cook for 4 minutes, turning once.

COOK'S TIP

Approximately half of the weight of flatfish is bone, so if buying your fish whole, ask the fishmonger to give you the correct weight of boned fish.

6 Toast and butter the muffins. Divide the fillets between them, top with spinach and a layer of mushrooms, then finish with a spoonful of crème fraîche or heavy cream.

Dover Sole in a Green Parsley Jacket

Quick to prepare and absolutely delicious, nothing compares with the rich sweetness of a Dover sole. Here, this fine fish sports a green parsley jacket trimmed with lemon and a hint of garlic.

Serves 2

INGREDIENTS
12 oz baking potatoes, peeled and finely chopped
1¼ cups milk, or as required
pinch of grated nutmeg
2 × Dover sole, skinned
2 tbsp butter
salt and freshly ground black pepper
lemon wedges, to serve

FOR THE PARSLEY JACKET
½ cup fresh parsley
1 oz crustless white bread, cubed
3 tbsp milk
2 tbsp olive oil
finely grated zest of ½ small lemon
1 small garlic clove, crushed

PREPARATION AND COOKING TIME
15 minutes

Dover sole

lemon

parsley

1 In a non-stick saucepan, cover the potatoes with the milk, add salt to taste, and the nutmeg, and bring to a boil. Simmer, uncovered, for 15 minutes until the potatoes have absorbed the milk. Mash, cover and keep warm.

2 To make the parsley jacket, chop the parsley in a food processor. Add the bread, milk, olive oil, lemon zest and garlic, then process to a fine paste.

3 Preheat a moderate broiler. Season the sole, dot with butter and broil for 5 minutes. Turn and allow 2 minutes on the other side. Spread with the parsley mixture, return to the broiler and continue to cook for a further 5 minutes. Serve with the mashed potatoes and wedges of lemon.

VARIATION

The same parsley mixture can be used to cover fillets of cod, haddock, whiting or flounder.

Salmon Risotto with Cucumber and Tarragon

Any rice can be used for risotto. The creamiest ones are made with short-grain Arborio and Carnaroli rice but they do take more time. Fresh tarragon and cucumber bring out the flavor of the salmon.

Serves 4

INGREDIENTS
2 tbsp butter
1 small bunch scallions, white part only, chopped
½ cucumber, peeled, deseeded and chopped
2 cups rice
3¾ cups fresh or canned chicken or fish stock
⅔ cup dry white wine
1 lb salmon fillet, skinned and diced
3 tbsp chopped fresh tarragon

PREPARATION AND COOKING TIME

20 minutes

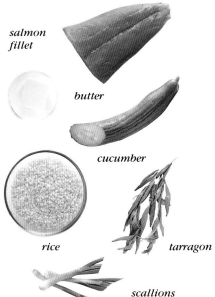

salmon fillet

butter

cucumber

rice

tarragon

scallions

1 Heat the butter in a large saucepan, and add the scallions and cucumber. Cook for 2–3 minutes without coloring.

2 Add the rice, stock and wine, return to a boil and simmer uncovered for 10 minutes, stirring occasionally.

3 Stir in the diced salmon and tarragon. Continue cooking for a further 5 minutes, then switch off the heat. Cover and leave to stand for 5 minutes before serving.

VARIATION

Long-grain rice can also be used. Choose grains that have not been pre-cooked and reduce the stock to 3⅔ cups, per 2 cups of rice.

Grilled Snapper with Hot Mango Salsa

A ripe mango provides the basis for a deliciously rich fruity salsa. The dressing needs no oil and features the tropical flavors of cilantro, ginger and chili.

VARIATION

If fresh mangoes are unavailable, use the canned variety and drain well. Sea bass are also good served with the hot mango salsa.

Serves 4

INGREDIENTS

12 oz new potatoes
3 eggs
4 oz green beans, topped, tailed and halved
4 × 12 oz red snapper, scaled and gutted
2 tbsp olive oil
6 oz mixed lettuce leaves, such as frisée or oak leaf
2 cherry tomatoes
salt and freshly ground black pepper

FOR THE SALSA

3 tbsp chopped fresh cilantro
1 medium sized ripe mango, peeled, pitted and diced
½ red chili, deseeded and chopped
1 in fresh ginger root, grated
juice of 2 limes
generous pinch of celery salt

PREPARATION AND COOKING TIME

20 minutes

green beans

red snapper

mango

ginger

chili

1 Bring the potatoes to a boil in a large saucepan of salted water and simmer for 15–20 minutes. Drain.

2 Bring a second large saucepan of salted water to a boil. Put in the eggs and boil for 4 minutes, then add the beans and cook for a further 6 minutes, so that the eggs have had a total of 10 minutes. Remove the eggs from the pan, cool, peel and cut into quarters.

3 Preheat a moderate broiler. Slash each snapper three times on either side, moisten with oil and cook for 12 minutes, turning once.

4 To make the dressing, place the cilantro in a food processor. Add the mango, chili, ginger, lime juice and celery salt and process smoothly.

5 Moisten the lettuce leaves with olive oil, and distribute them between four large plates.

6 Arrange the snapper over the lettuce and season to taste. Halve the new potatoes and tomatoes, and distribute them with the beans and quartered hard-boiled eggs over the salad. Serve with the salsa dressing.

Steaming Mussels with a Spicy Dipping Sauce

In this recipe, the mussel juices are thickened with split red lentils and spiced with curry.

Serves 4

INGREDIENTS
5 tbsp red lentils
2 loaves French bread
4 pints live mussels
5 tbsp white wine

FOR THE DIPPING SAUCE
2 tbsp vegetable oil
1 small onion, finely chopped
½ celery stalk, finely chopped
1 large garlic clove, crushed
1 tsp medium-hot curry paste

PREPARATION TIME
5 minutes

COOKING TIME
15 minutes

curry paste

French bread

garlic

red lentils

onion

celery

mussels

1 Soak the lentils in plenty of cold water until they are required. Preheat the oven to 300°F and put the bread in to warm. Clean the mussels in plenty of cold water and pull off any stray beards. Discard any that are damaged.

2 Place the mussels in a large saucepan. Add the white wine, cover and steam the mussels for 8 minutes.

3 Transfer the mussels to a colander over a bowl to collect the juices. Keep warm until required.

4 To make the dipping sauce, heat the vegetable oil in a second saucepan, add the onion and celery, and cook for 3–4 minutes to soften without coloring. Strain the mussel juices into a measuring cup to remove any sand or grit. There will be approximately 1⅔ cups of liquid.

5 Add the mussel juices to the saucepan, then add the garlic, curry paste and lentils. Bring to a boil and simmer for 10–12 minutes or until the lentils have fallen apart.

6 Turn the mussels out onto four serving plates and bring to the table with the dipping sauce, the warm French bread and a bowl to put the empty shells in.

Grilled Porgy with Fennel, Mustard and Orange

Porgy is a revelation to anyone unfamiliar with its creamy rich flavor. The fish has a firm white flesh that partners well with a rich butter sauce, sharpened here with a dash of frozen orange juice concentrate.

Serves 2

INGREDIENTS
2 baking potatoes
2 × 12 oz porgies, scaled and
   gutted
2 tsp Dijon mustard
1 tsp fennel seeds
2 tbsp olive oil
2 oz watercress
6 oz mixed lettuce leaves, such as
   curly endive or frisée

FOR THE SAUCE
2 tbsp frozen orange juice
   concentrate
¾ cup unsalted butter,
   diced
salt and cayenne pepper

PREPARATION AND COOKING TIME
20 minutes

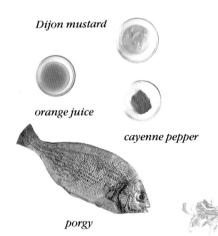

Dijon mustard

orange juice

cayenne pepper

porgy

lettuce

COOK'S TIP
For speedy baked potatoes, microwave small potatoes on 100% high power for 8 minutes, then crisp in a hot oven preheated to 400°F for a further 10 minutes. Split, butter and serve hot.

1 Cook the potatoes according to the tip at the beginning of this recipe. Preheat a moderate broiler. Slash the porgies four times on either side. Combine the mustard and fennel seeds, then spread over both sides of the fish. Moisten with oil and broil for 12 minutes, turning once.

2 Place the orange juice concentrate in a bowl and heat over 1 in of boiling water. Remove the pan from the stove, and gradually whisk the butter until creamy. Season, cover and set aside.

3 Moisten the watercress and lettuce leaves with the remaining olive oil, arrange the fish on two large plates and put the leaves to one side. Spoon over the sauce and serve with the potatoes.

Stir-fried Sweet and Sour Chicken

There are few cooking concepts that are better suited to today's busy lifestyle than the all-in-one stir-fry. This one has a South-east Asian influence.

Serves 4

INGREDIENTS
10 oz Chinese egg noodles
2 tbsp vegetable oil
3 scallions, chopped
1 garlic clove, crushed
1 in fresh ginger root, peeled and
   grated
1 tsp hot paprika
1 tsp ground coriander
3 boneless chicken breasts, sliced
1 cup sugar-snap peas, topped
   and tailed
4 oz baby corn, halved
8 oz fresh bean sprouts
1 tbsp cornstarch
3 tbsp soy sauce
3 tbsp lemon juice
1 tbsp sugar
3 tbsp chopped fresh cilantro or
   scallion tops, to garnish

PREPARATION AND COOKING TIME
15 minutes

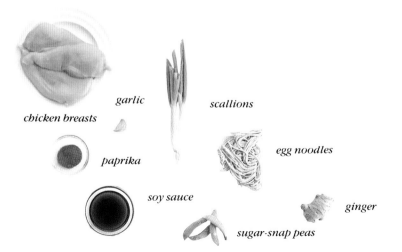

chicken breasts

garlic

scallions

paprika

egg noodles

soy sauce

sugar-snap peas

ginger

COOK'S TIP
Large wok lids are cumbersome and can be difficult to store in a small kitchen. Consider placing a circle of waxed paper against the food surface to keep cooking juices in.

1 Bring a large saucepan of salted water to a boil. Add the noodles and cook according to the package instructions. Drain, cover and keep warm.

2 Heat the oil. Add the scallions and cook over a gentle heat. Mix in the next five ingredients, then stir-fry for 3–4 minutes. Add the next three ingredients and steam briefly. Add the noodles.

3 Combine the cornstarch, soy sauce, lemon juice and sugar in a small bowl. Add to the wok and simmer briefly to thicken. Serve garnished with chopped cilantro or scallion tops.

Grilled Chicken with Pica de Gallo Salsa

This dish originates from Mexico. Its hot fruity flavors form the essence of Tex-Mex Cooking.

Serves 4

INGREDIENTS
4 chicken breasts
pinch of celery salt and cayenne
    pepper combined
2 tbsp vegetable oil
corn chips, to serve

FOR THE SALSA
10 oz watermelon
6 oz canteloupe melon
1 small red onion
1–2 green chilies
2 tbsp lime juice
4 tbsp chopped fresh cilantro
pinch of salt

PREPARATION TIME
5 minutes

COOKING TIME
15 minutes

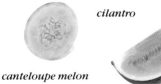

green chilies

chicken breasts

red onion

lime

cilantro

canteloupe melon

watermelon

COOK'S TIP

To capture the spirit of Tex-Mex food, cook the chicken over a barbecue and eat shaded from the hot summer sun.

1 Preheat a moderate broiler. Slash the chicken breasts deeply to speed up the cooking time.

2 Season the chicken with celery salt and cayenne, brush with oil and broil for about 15 minutes.

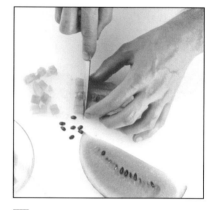

3 To make the salsa, remove the rind and as many seeds as you can from the melons. Finely dice the flesh and put it into a bowl.

4 Finely chop the onion, split the chilies (discarding the seeds which contain most of the heat) and chop. Take care not to touch sensitive skin areas when handling cut chilies. Mix with the melon.

5 Add the lime juice and chopped cilantro, and season with a pinch of salt. Turn the salsa into a small bowl.

6 Arrange the grilled chicken on a plate and serve with the salsa and a handful of corn chips.

Mexican Beef Burgers

Nothing beats the flavor and quality of a home-made burger. This version is from Mexico and is seasoned with cumin and fresh cilantro.

Makes 4

INGREDIENTS
4 ears of corn
1 cup stale white bread crumbs
6 tbsp milk
1 small onion, finely chopped
1 tsp ground cumin
½ tsp cayenne pepper
½ tsp celery salt
3 tbsp chopped fresh cilantro
2 lb lean ground beef
4 sesame buns
4 tbsp mayonnaise
4 tomato slices
½ iceberg lettuce or other leaves
   such as frisée or Romaine
salt and freshly ground black pepper
1 large packet corn chips,
   to serve

PREPARATION TIME
10 minutes

COOKING TIME
10 minutes

ground beef
iceberg lettuce

onion

tomatoes
sesame buns

white bread

1 Bring a large saucepan of water to a boil, add a good pinch of salt and cook the corn for 15 minutes.

2 Combine the bread crumbs, milk, onion, cumin, cayenne, celery salt and fresh cilantro in a large bowl.

3 Add the beef and mix by hand until evenly blended.

4 Divide the beef mixture into four portions and flatten between sheets of plastic wrap.

5 Preheat a moderate broiler and cook for 10 minutes for medium burgers or 15 minutes for well-done burgers, turning once during the cooking time.

6 Split and toast the buns, spread with mayonnaise and sandwich the burgers with the tomato slices, lettuce leaves and seasoning. Serve with corn chips and the ears of corn.

COOK'S TIP

If planning ahead, freeze the burgers between sheets of wax paper or plastic wrap. Covered, they will keep well for up to twelve weeks. Defrost before cooking.

Black Pepper Beef Steaks with Red Wine Sauce

Every cook should know how to rustle up a pan-steak dinner with an impressive sauce to go with it. Black peppercorns follow the French tradition and combine well with the other bold flavors in the sauce.

Serves 4

INGREDIENTS
12 oz frozen fried potatoes or
   4 baking potatoes
1 tbsp black peppercorns
4 × 8 oz sirloin steaks
1 tbsp olive oil
chopped fresh parsley, to garnish
5 oz green salad, to serve

FOR THE RED WINE SAUCE
½ cup red wine
3 oz field mushrooms, sliced
¼ oz dried morel mushrooms, soaked
   (optional)
1¼ cups beef stock
1 tbsp cornstarch
1 tsp Dijon mustard
½ tsp anchovy paste (optional)
2 tsp red wine vinegar
2 tbsp butter
salt and freshly ground black pepper

PREPARATION AND COOKING TIME
20 minutes

cornstarch

dried morel mushrooms

anchovy paste

sirloin steaks

wine vinegar

peppercorns

Dijon mustard

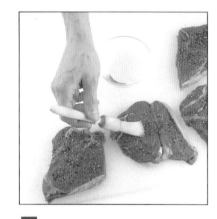

1 Preheat the oven according to the instructions on the package for frozen fried potatoes and cook. Alternatively, if you require baked potatoes, cook in the microwave on high power (100%) for 8 minutes and then place in a preheated oven at 375°F for a further 10 minutes. Crush the peppercorns using a pestle and mortar, or coarsely grind in a pepper mill. Coat both sides of the steak with the crushed peppercorns and brush lightly with olive oil.

2 Heat a heavy bare metal frying pan. Fry the steaks for 6–8 minutes for medium-rare or 12–16 minutes for well-done steaks, turning once throughout the cooking time.

3 Transfer the steaks to a plate, cover and keep warm. Pour off the excess fat from the frying pan, return to the heat and brown the sediment. To make the sauce, add the wine and stir with a flat wooden spoon to loosen the sediment.

4 Add the mushrooms to the frying pan with the dried morels, if using. Pour in the stock and cook briefly to soften.

5 Measure the cornstarch, mustard and anchovy paste, if using, into a small bowl. Add 2 tbsp of water and blend together to a smooth paste. Add to the pan, stirring continuously, and simmer to thicken.

COOK'S TIP

Non-stick frying pans are not suitable for making pan sauces. Only bare metal pans allow a rich sediment to form, which is essential to the flavor of a good sauce.

6 Add the vinegar to taste. Toss in the butter and swirl the contents in the pan with a circular motion until the butter has melted. Season to taste, return the steaks and heat through. Arrange the steaks on four plates, pour over the sauce and sprinkle with parsley. Serve with fries or baked potatoes and a green salad.

Lamb Chop Sauté with a Rich Pan Sauce

When lamb is sautéed in a heavy pan, a delicious sauce can be made from the sediment left behind.

Serves 4

INGREDIENTS

1½ lb new potatoes
4 × 6 oz loin lamb chops, or leg steaks
1 tbsp olive oil
3 fresh rosemary sprigs
5 tbsp red wine
scant 1 cup fresh or canned chicken
    stock
2 tsp cornstarch
½ tsp black olive paste (optional)
2 tsp white wine vinegar
2 tbsp unsalted butter
salt and freshly ground black pepper
carrots and petit pois, to serve

PREPARATION AND COOKING TIME

20 minutes

olive paste

lamb chops

Dijon mustard

red wine

black pepper

butter

rosemary

1 Bring the potatoes to a boil in a large saucepan of salted water and simmer for 15–20 minutes. Season the lamb with pepper and moisten with oil. Heat a large bare metal frying pan on the stove, add the rosemary and lay the meat over the top. Allow 6–8 minutes for medium-rare or 12–15 minutes for well-done lamb, turning once during the cooking time. Transfer to a warm plate, cover and allow the juices to settle.

2 Pour off any excess oil and discard the rosemary. Return the frying pan to the stove and heat the sediment until it browns. Add the wine and stir to loosen with a flat wooden spoon. Pour in the chicken stock and simmer.

3 Combine the cornstarch, mustard and olive paste, if using, in a small bowl, adding 1 tbsp of cold water to soften. Stir the contents of the bowl into the frying pan and simmer briefly to thicken. Add the vinegar, then stir in the butter. Arrange the potatoes, carrots, petit pois and lamb chops on four plates, pour over the sauce and serve.

Indonesian Pork and Peanut Saté

These delicious skewers of pork are popular street food in Indonesia. They are quick to make and eat.

Serves 4

INGREDIENTS
2 cups long-grain rice
1 lb lean pork
pinch of salt
2 limes, quartered, to garnish
4 oz green salad, to serve

FOR THE BASTE AND DIP
1 tbsp vegetable oil
1 small onion, chopped
1 garlic clove, crushed
½ tsp hot chili sauce
1 tbsp sugar
2 tbsp soy sauce
2 tbsp lemon or lime juice
½ tsp anchovy paste (optional)
4 tbsp smooth peanut butter

PREPARATION TIME

10 minutes

COOKING TIME

10 minutes

lemon

lime

rice

peanut butter

pork

garlic

chili sauce

1 In a large saucepan, cover the rice with 3¾ cups of boiling salted water, stir and simmer uncovered for 15 minutes until the liquid has been absorbed. Switch off the heat, cover and stand for 5 minutes. Slice the pork into thin strips, then thread zig-zag fashion onto 16 bamboo skewers.

2 Heat the vegetable oil in a pan. Add the onion and cook over a gentle heat to soften without coloring for about 3–4 minutes. Add the next 5 ingredients and the anchovy paste, if using. Simmer briefly, then stir in the peanut butter

3 Preheat a moderate broiler, spoon a third of the sauce over the pork and cook for 6–8 minutes, turning once. Spread the rice out onto a serving dish, place the pork saté on top and serve with the dipping sauce. Garnish with quartered limes and serve with a green salad.

VARIATION
Indonesian saté can be prepared with lean beef, chicken or shrimp.

Pan-fried Pork with Peaches and Green Peppercorns

When peaches are in season, consider this speedy pork dish, brought alive with green peppercorns.

Serves 4

INGREDIENTS

2 cups long-grain rice
4 cups chicken stock
4 × 7 oz pork chops or
   loin pieces
2 tbsp vegetable oil
2 tbsp dark rum or sherry
1 small onion, chopped
3 large ripe peaches
1 tbsp green peppercorns
1 tbsp white wine vinegar
salt and freshly ground black pepper

PREPARATION AND COOKING TIME

20 minutes

onion

pork chops

dark rum

oil

green peppercorns

white wine vinegar

peaches

1 Cover the rice with 3¾ cups chicken stock. Stir, bring to a simmer and cook uncovered for 15 minutes. Switch off the heat and cover for 5 minutes. Season the pork with a generous twist of black pepper. Heat a large bare metal frying pan and moisten the pork with 1 tbsp of the oil. Cook the pork for 12 minutes, turning once.

4 Cover the peaches with boiling water to loosen the skins, then peel, slice and discard the pits.

2 Transfer the meat to a warm plate. Pour off the excess fat from the pan and return to the heat. Allow the sediment to sizzle and brown, add the rum or sherry and loosen the sediment with a flat wooden spoon. Pour the pan contents over the meat, cover and keep warm. Wipe the pan clean.

5 Add the peaches and peppercorns to the onion and coat for 3–4 minutes, until they begin to soften.

VARIATION

If peaches are not ripe when picked, they can be difficult to peel. Only tree ripened fruit is suitable for peeling. If fresh peaches are out of season, a can of sliced peaches may be used instead.

3 Heat the remaining vegetable oil in the pan and soften the onion over a steady heat.

6 Add the remaining chicken stock and simmer briefly. Return the pork and meat juices to the pan, sharpen with vinegar, and season to taste. Serve with the rice.

Sausage Popovers

This quick and filling dish is similar to Toad in the Hole, and is always well received.

Serves 4

INGREDIENTS
2 lb baking potatoes
1 lb pork or beef sausages or
   chipolatas
1 × 14 oz can petit pois, to serve
   (optional)

FOR THE BATTER
3 eggs
1¼ cups whole milk
1 cup flour
salt and freshly ground black pepper

FOR THE ONION GRAVY
2 tbsp vegetable oil
1 medium onion, chopped
1 tbsp flour
scant 1 cup fresh or canned chicken
   or beef stock
1 tsp balsamic or red wine
   vinegar

PREPARATION TIME

10 minutes

COOKING TIME

10 minutes

onion

eggs

flour

sausages

1 Cut the potatoes into small pieces to reduce the cooking time. Bring them to a boil in salted water and cook for 15 minutes. Preheat the oven to 450°F and partly cook the sausages or chipolatas for 5 minutes.

2 To make the batter, beat the eggs together with a good pinch of salt and a twist of black pepper in a bowl.

3 Add half of the milk and all of the flour and stir into a smooth batter. Pour in the remaining milk and combine evenly.

4 Arrange the partly cooked sausages in a shallow muffin tin.

5 Pour in the batter, transfer to the preheated oven and bake for 10 minutes until well risen and golden.

COOK'S TIP
When making risen batter dishes, it is important to put the mixture into a fiercely hot oven.

6 To make the onion gravy, heat the vegetable oil in a large saucepan and brown the onion for 3–4 minutes, then add the flour. Remove from the heat, gradually stir in the stock and sharpen with vinegar to taste. Mash the potatoes and serve with the popovers, gravy and petit pois if desired.

Wild Mushroom Rösti with Bacon and Eggs

Dried ceps or porcini mushrooms, commonly found in Italian delicatessens, are a good substitute for fresh. Cook them in a potato rösti and serve with bacon and a fried egg for breakfast or a lazy supper.

Serves 4

INGREDIENTS

1 ½ lb baking potatoes, peeled
¼ oz dried ceps or porcini
   mushrooms
2 fresh thyme sprigs, chopped
2 tbsp chopped fresh parsley
4 tbsp vegetable oil, for frying
4 × 4 oz unsmoked bacon
pinch of salt
4 eggs, to serve
1 bunch watercress or flat-leaf parsley,
   to serve

PREPARATION AND COOKING TIME

20 minutes

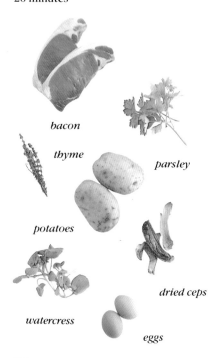

bacon

thyme

parsley

potatoes

dried ceps

watercress

eggs

COOK'S TIP

A large rösti can be made in a non-stick frying pan. Allow 12 minutes to cook. Half-way through the cooking time, invert the rösti on a large plate and slide back into the pan.

1 Bring the potatoes to a boil in a pan of salted water and cook for 5 minutes.

2 Cover the mushrooms with boiling water to soften, then chop roughly.

3 Drain the potatoes, allow them to cool and grate them coarsely. Add the mushrooms, thyme and parsley and combine together well.

4 Heat 2 tbsp of the oil in a frying pan, spoon in the rösti mixture in heaps and flatten. Fry for 6 minutes, turning once during cooking.

5 Preheat a moderate broiler and cook the bacon slices until sizzling.

6 Heat the remaining oil in a frying pan and fry the eggs as you like them. Serve the rösti together with the eggs and bacon and a watercress salad.

Jambalaya

The perfect way to use up left-over cold meat –
Jambalaya is a fast, fortifying meal for a hungry family.

Serves 4

INGREDIENTS
3 tbsp vegetable oil
1 medium onion, chopped
1 celery stalk, chopped
½ red bell pepper, chopped
2 cups long-grain rice
4 cups fresh or canned chicken stock
1 tbsp tomato paste
3–4 shakes of Tabasco sauce
8 oz cold roast chicken or pork,
   thickly sliced
4 oz cooked sausage, such as chorizo
   or kabanos, sliced
¾ cup frozen peas

PREPARATION AND COOKING TIME

20 minutes

roast chicken

peas

tomato paste

onion

sausages

celery

red bell pepper

rice

1 Heat the oil in a heavy saucepan and add the onion, celery and pepper. Cook to soften without coloring.

2 Add the rice, chicken stock, tomato paste and Tabasco sauce. Simmer uncovered for 10 minutes.

3 Stir in the cold meat, sausage and peas and simmer for a further 5 minutes. Switch off the heat, cover and leave to stand for 5 minutes more before serving.

VARIATION
You could also add cooked ham, smoked cod or haddock and fresh shellfish to a Jambalaya.

Gorgonzola, Cauliflower and Walnut Gratin

This cauliflower dish is covered with a bubbly blue cheese sauce topped with chopped walnuts and cooked under the broiler

Serves 4

INGREDIENTS

1 large cauliflower, broken into florets
2 tbsp butter
1 medium onion, finely chopped
3 tbsp flour
scant 2 cups milk
5 oz Gorgonzola or other blue cheese, cut into pieces
½ tsp celery salt
pinch of cayenne papper
¾ cup chopped walnuts
pinch of salt
fresh parsley, to garnish
4 oz green salad, to serve

PREPARATION TIME

10 minutes

COOKING TIME

10 minutes

onion

Gorgonzola

butter

walnuts

cauliflower

1 Bring a large saucepan of salted water to a boil and cook the cauliflower for 6 minutes. Drain and place in a flameproof gratin dish.

2 Heat the butter in a heavy saucepan. Add the onion and cook over a gentle heat to soften without coloring. Stir in the flour, then remove from the heat. Stir in the milk a little at a time until absorbed by the flour, stirring continuously. Add the cheese, celery salt and cayenne pepper. Simmer and stir to thicken.

3 Preheat a moderate broiler. Spoon the sauce over the cauliflower, scatter with chopped walnuts and broil until golden. Garnish with the parsley and serve with a crisp green salad.

VARIATION

For a delicious alternative, substitute cauliflower with 2½ lb fresh broccoli or combine both together.

Risotto-stuffed Eggplants with Spicy Tomato Sauce

Eggplants are a challenge to the creative cook and allow for some unusual recipe ideas. Here, they are stuffed and baked with a cheese and pine nut topping.

Serves 4

INGREDIENTS
4 small eggplants
7 tbsp olive oil
1 small onion, chopped
scant 1 cup arborio rice
3²⁄₃ cups ready-made or fresh
    vegetable stock
1 tbsp white wine vinegar
8 fresh basil sprigs, to garnish

FOR THE TOPPING
¼ cup freshly grated Parmesan
    cheese
1 tbsp pine nuts

FOR THE TOMATO SAUCE
1¼ cups crushed tomatoes or
tomato purée
1 tsp mild curry paste
pinch of salt

PREPARATION AND COOKING TIME
20 minutes

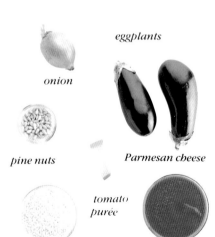

eggplants

onion

pine nuts

Parmesan cheese

tomato purée

COOK'S TIP
Don't be put off by the amount of oil eggplants absorb when cooking. Use olive oil and remember that good oils are low in saturated fat and are believed to fight against heart disease.

1 Preheat the oven to 400°F. Cut the eggplants in half lengthwise and take out their flesh with a small knife. Brush with 2 tbsp of the oil, place on a baking sheet and cook in the preheated oven for 6–8 minutes.

2 Chop the reserved eggplant flesh and heat the remainder of the olive oil in a medium saucepan. Add the eggplant flesh and the onion and cook over a gentle heat for 3–4 minutes until soft.

3 Add the rice, stir in the stock and simmer uncovered for a further 15 minutes. Stir in the vinegar.

4 Increase the oven temperature to 450°F. Spoon the rice into the eggplant skins, top with cheese and pine nuts, and return to the oven to brown for 5 minutes.

5 To make the sauce, combine the crushed tomatoes or tomato purée with the curry paste, heat and add salt to taste.

6 Spoon the sauce onto four large serving plates and position two eggplant halves on each. Garnish with basil sprigs.

Spanish Omelet

Spanish omelet belongs in every cook's repertoire and can vary according to what you have in store. This version includes white beans and is finished with a layer of toasted sesame seeds.

Serves 4

INGREDIENTS
2 tbsp olive oil
1 tsp sesame oil
1 Spanish onion, chopped
1 small red bell pepper, deseeded and diced
2 celery stalks, chopped
1 × 14 oz can soft white beans, drained
8 eggs
3 tbsp sesame seeds
salt and freshly ground black pepper
4 oz green salad, to serve

PREPARATION TIME

10 minutes

COOKING TIME

10 minutes

celery

red bell pepper

white beans

sesame oil

sesame seeds

eggs

VARIATION

You can also use sliced cooked potatoes, any seasonal vegetables, baby artichoke hearts and chick-peas in a Spanish omelet.

1 Heat the olive and sesame oils in a 12 in paella or frying pan. Add the onion, pepper and celery and cook to soften without coloring.

2 Add the beans and continue to cook for several minutes to heat through.

3 In a small bowl beat the eggs with a fork, season well and pour over the ingredients in the pan.

4 Stir the egg mixture with a flat wooden spoon until it begins to stiffen, then allow to firm over a low heat for about 6–8 minutes.

5 Preheat a moderate broiler. Sprinkle the omelette with sesame seeds and brown evenly under the broiler.

6 Cut the omelet into thick wedges and serve warm with a green salad.

Omelet aux Fines Herbs

Eggs respond well to fast cooking and combine beautifully with a handful of fresh herbs. Serve with French fries and a green salad.

Serves 1

INGREDIENTS
3 eggs
2 tbsp chopped fresh parsley
2 tbsp chopped fresh chervil
2 tbsp chopped fresh tarragon
1 tbsp chopped fresh chives
1 tbsp butter
salt and freshly ground black pepper
12 oz frozen French fries,
    to serve
4 oz green salad, to serve
1 tomato, to serve

PREPARATION AND COOKING TIME

15 minutes

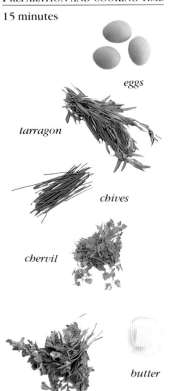

eggs

tarragon

chives

chervil

parsley

butter

1 Break the eggs into a bowl, season to taste and beat with a fork, then add the chopped herbs.

2 Heat an omelet or frying pan over a high heat, add the butter and cook until it foams and browns. Quickly pour in the beaten egg and stir briskly with the back of the fork. When the egg is two-thirds scrambled, let the omelet finish cooking for 10–15 seconds more.

3 Tap the handle of the omelet or frying pan sharply with your fist to make the omelet jump up the sides of the pan, fold and turn onto a plate. Serve with French fries, green salad and a halved tomato.

COOK'S TIP

From start to finish, an omelet should be cooked and on the table in less than a minute. For best results use free-range eggs at room temperature.

Mushroom Macaroni and Cheese

Macaroni cheese is an all-time classic from the mid-week menu. Here it is served in a light creamy sauce with mushrooms and topped with pine nuts.

Serves 4

INGREDIENTS

1 lb quick-cooking elbow macaroni
3 tbsp olive oil
8 oz field mushrooms, sliced
2 fresh thyme sprigs
4 tbsp plain flour
1 vegetable bouillon cube
2½ cups milk
½ tsp celery salt
1 tsp Dijon mustard
1½ cups grated Cheddar cheese
¼ cup freshly grated Parmesan cheese
2 tbsp pine nuts
salt and freshly ground black pepper

PREPARATION AND COOKING TIME

20 minutes

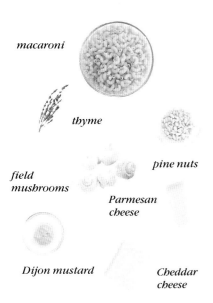

macaroni

thyme

pine nuts

field mushrooms

Parmesan cheese

Dijon mustard

Cheddar cheese

1 Bring a pan of salted water to a boil. Add the macaroni and cook according to the package instructions.

2 Heat the oil in a heavy saucepan. Add the mushrooms and thyme, cover and cook over a gentle heat for 2–3 minutes. Stir in the flour and draw from the heat, add the bouillon cube and stir continuously until evenly blended. Add the milk a little at a time, stirring after each addition. Add the celery salt, mustard and Cheddar cheese and season. Stir and simmer briefly for 1–2 minutes.

3 Preheat a moderate broiler. Drain the macaroni well, toss into the sauce and turn out into four individual dishes or one large flameproof gratin dish. Scatter with grated Parmesan cheese and pine nuts, then broil until brown and bubbly.

COOK'S TIP

Tightly closed mushrooms are best for white cream sauces. Open mushrooms can darken a pale sauce to an unattractive sludgy grey.

Red Bell Pepper Polenta with Sunflower Salsa

This recipe is inspired by Italian and Mexican cookery. Cornmeal polenta is a staple food in Italy, served with brightly colored vegetables. Mexican *Pipian* is a salsa made from sunflower seeds, chili and lime.

Serves 4

INGREDIENTS
3 young zucchinis
oil, for greasing
5 cups light vegetable
   stock
2 cups fine polenta or
   cornmeal
1 × 7 oz jar red peppers, drained
   and sliced
4 oz green salad, to serve

FOR THE SUNFLOWER SALSA
3 oz sunflower seeds, toasted
1 cup crustless white
   bread
scant 1 cup vegetable
   stock
1 garlic clove, crushed
½ red chili, deseeded and chopped
2 tbsp chopped fresh cilantro
1 tsp sugar
1 tbsp lime juice
pinch of salt

PREPARATION AND COOKING TIME

20 minutes

1 Bring a saucepan of salted water to a boil. Add the zucchinis and simmer over a low heat for 2–3 minutes. Refresh under cold running water and drain. When they are cool, cut into strips.

2 Lightly oil a 9 in loaf pan and line with a single sheet of waxed paper.

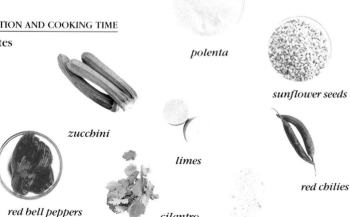

polenta

sunflower seeds

zucchini

limes

red chilies

red bell peppers

cilantro

white bread

3 Bring the vegetable stock to a simmer in a heavy saucepan. Add the polenta in a steady stream, stirring continuously for about 2–3 minutes until thickened.

4 Partly fill the lined pan with the polenta mixture. Layer the sliced zucchinis and peppers over the polenta. Fill the pan with the remaining polenta and leave to set for about 10–15 minutes. Polenta should be served warm or at room temperature.

COOK'S TIP

Sunflower salsa will keep for up to 10 days in the refrigerator. It is delicious poured over a simple dish of pasta.

5 To make the salsa, grind the sunflower seeds to a thick paste in a food processor. Add the remaining ingredients and combine thoroughly.

6 Turn the warm polenta out onto a board, remove the paper and cut into thick slices with a large wet knife. Serve with the salsa and a green salad.

Spinach and Ricotta Shells with Pine Nuts

Large pasta shells are designed to hold a variety of delicious stuffings. Few are more pleasing than this mixture of chopped spinach and ricotta cheese.

COOK'S TIP
Choose a large saucepan when cooking pasta and give it an occasional stir to prevent shapes from sticking together. You can use either crushed tomatoes or tomato purée.

Serves 4

INGREDIENTS

12 oz large pasta shells
scant 2 cups crushed tomatoes or
    tomato purée
10 oz frozen chopped spinach,
    defrosted
2 oz crustless white bread, crumbled
½ cup milk
3 tbsp olive oil
2¼ cups ricotta cheese
pinch of nutmeg
1 garlic clove, crushed
1 tbsp olive oil
½ tsp black olive paste (optional)
¼ cup freshly grated Parmesan
    cheese
2 tbsp pine nuts
salt and freshly ground black pepper

PREPARATION AND COOKING TIME

20 minutes

olive paste

ricotta cheese

pine nuts

garlic

spinach   pasta shells

1 Bring a large saucepan of salted water to a boil. Toss in the pasta and cook according to the directions on the package. Refresh under cold water, drain and reserve until needed.

2 Pour the crushed tomatoes or purée into a nylon sieve over a bowl and strain to thicken. Place the spinach in another sieve and press out any excess liquid with the back of a spoon.

3 Place the bread, milk and oil in a food processor and combine. Add the spinach and ricotta and season with salt, pepper and nutmeg.

4 Combine the crushed tomatoes with the garlic, olive oil and olive paste if using. Spread the sauce evenly over the bottom of an ovenproof dish.

5 Spoon the spinach mixture into a piping bag fitted with a large plain nozzle and fill the pasta shapes (alternatively fill with a spoon). Arrange the pasta shapes over the sauce.

6 Preheat a moderate broiler. Heat the pasta through in a microwave oven at high power (100%) for 4 minutes. Scatter with Parmesan cheese and pine nuts, and finish under the broiler to brown the cheese.

Pasta Rapido with Parsley Pesto

Pasta suppers can often be dull. Here's a fresh, lively sauce that will stir the appetite.

Serves 4

INGREDIENTS
1 lb dried pasta
¾ cup whole almonds
½ cup slivered almonds, toasted
¼ cup freshly grated Parmesan
   cheese
pinch of salt

FOR THE SAUCE
1½ oz fresh parsley
2 garlic cloves, crushed
3 tbsp olive oil
3 tbsp lemon juice
1 tsp sugar
1 cup boiling water

PREPARATION AND COOKING TIME

20 minutes

pasta

lemon

parsley

garlic

Parmesan cheese

slivered almonds

almonds

1 Bring a large saucepan of salted water to a boil. Toss in the pasta and cook according to the instructions on the package. Toast the whole and slivered almonds separately under a moderate broiler until golden brown. Put the slivered almonds aside until required.

2 For the sauce, chop the parsley finely in a food processor. Add the whole almonds and grind to a fine consistency. Add the garlic, olive oil, lemon juice, sugar and water. Combine to make a sauce.

3 Drain the pasta and combine with half of the sauce. (The remainder of the sauce will keep in a screw-topped jar in the refrigerator for up to ten days.) Top with Parmesan and slivered almonds.

COOK'S TIP

To prevent pasta from sticking together during cooking, use plenty of water and stir well before the water returns to a boil.

Succotash Soup Plate

Succotash is a North American Indian dish of corn and lima beans. Originally the dish was enriched with bear fat, although modern day succotash is finished with milk or cream. This version makes an appetizing and filling main course soup.

Serves 4

INGREDIENTS

4 tbsp butter
1 large onion, chopped
2 large carrots, peeled and cut into
    short sticks
3¾ cups milk
1 vegetable bouillon cube
2 medium-sized waxy potatoes,
    peeled and diced
1 thyme sprig
2 cups frozen corn
3 cups frozen lima beans or broad
    beans
2 tbsp chopped fresh parsley,
    to garnish

PREPARATION AND COOKING TIME

20 minutes

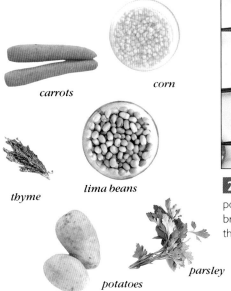

carrots *corn*

thyme *lima beans*

potatoes *parsley*

1 Heat the butter in a large saucepan. Add the onion and carrots and cook over a gentle heat for 3–4 minutes, to soften without coloring.

2 Add the milk, bouillon cube, potatoes, thyme, corn and lima beans or broad beans. Simmer for 10 minutes until the potatoes are cooked through.

COOK'S TIP

Frozen corn and lima beans are best for flavor and convenience in this soup, although the canned variety may also be used.

3 Season to taste, ladle into soup plates and garnish with chopped fresh parsley.

Caponata

Caponata is a quintessential part of Sicilian antipasti and is a rich, spicy mixture of eggplants, tomatoes, capers and celery.

Serves 4

INGREDIENTS

4 tbsp olive oil
1 large onion, sliced
2 celery stalks, sliced
1 lb eggplant, diced
5 ripe tomatoes, chopped
1 garlic clove, crushed
3 tbsp red wine vinegar
1 tbsp sugar
2 tbsp capers
12 olives
pinch of salt
4 tbsp chopped fresh parsley,
   to garnish
warm crusty bread, to serve
olives, to serve

PREPARATION TIME

10 minutes

COOKING TIME

10 minutes

celery

eggplants

onion

tomatoes

olives

capers

1 Heat half the oil in a large heavy saucepan. Add the onion and celery and cook over a gentle heat for about 3–4 minutes to soften.

2 Add the remainder of the oil with the eggplants and stir to absorb the oil. Cook until the eggplants begin to color, then add the chopped tomatoes, garlic, vinegar and sugar.

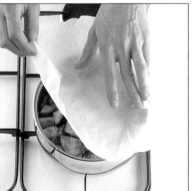

3 Cover the surface of the vegetables with a circle of waxed paper and simmer for 8–10 minutes.

4 Add the capers and olives, then season to taste with salt. Turn the caponata out into a bowl, garnish with parsley and serve at room temperature with warm crusty bread and olives.

Red Berry Sponge Tart

When soft berry fruits are in season, try making this delicious sponge tart. Serve warm from the oven with scoops of vanilla ice cream.

Serves 4

INGREDIENTS
softened butter, for greasing
4 cups soft berry fruits such as
    raspberries, blackberries, black
    currants, red currants, strawberries
    or blueberries
2 eggs, at room temperature
¼ cup superfine sugar, plus extra to
    taste (optional)
1 tbsp flour
¾ cup ground almonds
vanilla ice cream, to serve

PREPARATION TIME
5 minutes

COOKING TIME
15 minutes

eggs

ground almonds

flour   *superfine sugar*
red currants

black currants

raspberries   *strawberries*

1 Preheat the oven to 375°F. Brush a 9 in pic pan with softened butter and line the bottom with a circle of non-stick baking paper. Scatter the fruit in the bottom of the pan with a little sugar if the fruits are tart.

2 Whisk the eggs and sugar together for about 3–4 minutes or until they leave a thick trail across the surface. Combine the flour and almonds, then fold into the egg mixture with a spatula – retaining as much air as possible.

3 Spread the mixture on top of the fruit base and bake in the preheated oven for 15 minutes. Turn out onto a serving plate and serve with vanilla ice cream.

VARIATION
When berry fruits are out of season, use bottled fruits, but ensure that they are well drained before use.

Raspberry and Passionfruit Puffs

Few desserts are so strikingly easy to make as this one: beaten egg whites and sugar baked in a dish, turned out and served with a handful of soft fruit.

Serves 4

INGREDIENTS
2 tbsp butter, softened
5 egg whites
⅔ cup superfine sugar
2 passionfruit
1 cup ready-made custard from a
    carton or can
milk, as required
6 cups fresh raspberries
confectioners' sugar, for dusting

PREPARATION TIME
10 minutes

COOKING TIME
10 minutes

raspberries

egg whites

passionfruit

confectioners' sugar

VARIATION
If raspberries are out of season, use either fresh, bottled or canned soft berry fruit such as strawberries, blueberries or red currants.

1 Preheat the oven to 350°F. Brush four ½ pint soufflé dishes with a visible layer of soft butter.

2 Whisk the egg whites in a mixing bowl until firm. (You can use an electric mixer.) Add the sugar a little at a time and whisk into a firm meringue.

3 Halve the passionfruit, take out the seeds with a spoon and fold them into the meringue.

4 Turn the meringue out into the prepared dishes, stand in a deep roasting pan which has been half-filled with boiling water and bake for 10 minutes. The meringue will rise above the tops of the soufflé dishes.

5 Turn the puffs out upside-down onto a serving plate.

6 Top with raspberries. Thin the custard with a little milk and pour around the edge. Dredge with confectioners' sugar and serve warm or cold.

Chocolate Mousse on the Loose

Super-light, dark, creamy and delicious; the chocolate mousse is always popular and should maintain a high profile on any dessert menu.

Serves 4

INGREDIENTS

7 oz best quality plain chocolate, plus
  extra for flaking
3 eggs
2 tbsp dark rum or whisky
¼ cup superfine sugar
½ pint/1¼ cups whipping
  cream
confectioners' sugar, for dusting

PREPARATION TIME

15 minutes

plain chocolate

whipping cream

eggs

superfine sugar

1 Break the chocolate into a bowl, stand over a saucepan of simmering water and melt. Separate the egg whites into a large mixing bowl, remove the chocolate from the heat and stir in the egg yolks and alcohol.

2 Whisk the egg whites until firm, gradually add the sugar and whisk until stiff peaks form.

3 Whip the cream to a dropping consistency and set aside until required.

4 Give the egg whites a final beating with a rubber spatula, add the chocolate and fold all the ingredients together gently, retaining as much air as possible.

5 Fold in the loosely whipped cream, turn into four glasses or bowls and chill until ready to serve.

COOK'S TIP

It is a false economy to use inexpensive chocolate. Choose the best quality dark chocolate you can find and enjoy it!

6 Decorate with flaked chocolate and dust with confectioners' sugar.

Ice Cream Strawberry Shortcake

This simple dessert is an all-time American classic. Make sure you use the freshest, most beautiful berries available. You can substitute whipped cream for the ice cream if you like.

Serves 4

INGREDIENTS
3 × 6 in ready-made sponge cake
  cases or shortcakes
2 pints/5 cups vanilla or strawberry
  ice cream
1 ½ lb hulled fresh strawberries
confectioners' sugar, for dusting

PREPARATION TIME
10 minutes

strawberries

confectioners sugar

sponge cake case

1 If using sponge cake cases, trim the raised edges with a serrated knife.

2 Sandwich the sponge cake cases or shortcakes with two-thirds of the ice cream and the strawberries.

3 Place the remaining ice cream on top, finish with strawberries, dust with confectioners' sugar and serve.

COOK'S TIP

Don't worry if the shortcake falls apart when you cut into it. Messy cakes are best. Ice Cream Strawberry Shortcake can be assembled up to 1 hour in advance and kept in the freezer without spoiling the fruit.

Kentucky Fried Peaches

Never mind your diet, when peaches are this good, it's time for a break!

Serves 4

INGREDIENTS
5 large ripe peaches
4 tbsp butter
2 tbsp brown sugar
3 tbsp Kentucky bourbon
2 pints/5 cups vanilla ice
 cream
½ cup pecan nuts, toasted

PREPARATION TIME

5 minutes

COOKING TIME

10 minutes

vanilla ice cream

pecan nuts

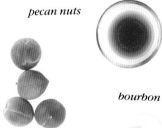

bourbon

peaches

butter

brown sugar

COOK'S TIP
Peaches that ripen after they are picked will not release their skins when blanched in boiling water.

1 Place the peaches in a large bowl and cover with boiling water to loosen their skins. Drain, refresh under cold running water and slice.

2 Heat the butter in a large frying pan until it foams and begins to brown. Add the sugar, peaches and bourbon, turn up the heat and cook until soft and syrupy. Spoon the hot peaches over the ice cream and decorate with pecan nuts.

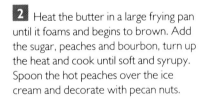

Apricot and Almond Bake

This dessert consists of a few apricots, either fresh or canned, strewn over an almond batter. Hot from the oven, this dessert is bound to please with a scoop or two of best vanilla ice cream.

Serves 4

INGREDIENTS
4 tbsp butter, softened, plus extra for
    greasing
¼ cup superfine sugar
¾ ground almonds
1 tbsp self-rising flour
1 egg
½ tsp almond extract
1 cup fresh apricots or 1 × 14 oz can
    apricots in syrup
confectioners' sugar, for dusting
vanilla ice cream, custard or cream,
    to serve

PREPARATION TIME

10 minutes

COOKING TIME

10 minutes

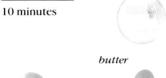

butter

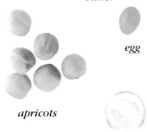

egg

apricots

flour

ground almonds

superfine sugar

COOK'S TIP
Metal pie plates are preferable to porcelain or pottery because they are better conductors of heat and will reduce the cooking time.

1 Preheat the oven to 400°F. Lightly grease a 9 in enamel pie plate with butter and set aside.

2 Soften the butter if necessary in a microwave oven for 20 seconds at 100% high power. Combine the butter and sugar in a mixing bowl.

3 Mix the ground almonds and flour together and add to the butter.

4 Add the egg and almond extract, then combine into a smooth batter.

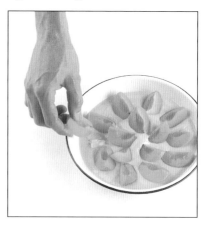

5 Turn the batter into a pie plate and spread it to the edge. Split the apricots, peel and discard the pits if using fresh fruit, and arrange over the batter. Bake in the preheated oven for 15–20 minutes until springy to the touch.

6 Dust with sugar and serve hot with vanilla ice cream, cream or custard.

Black Forest Sundae

Here is a variation on the classic Black Forest Gâteau, served in a sundae glass.

Serves 4

INGREDIENTS
1 × 14 oz can pitted black cherries in syrup
1 tbsp cornstarch
3 tbsp kirsch
⅔ cup heavy or whipping cream
1 tbsp confectioners' sugar
1 pint/2½ cups chocolate ice cream
4 oz chocolate cake
8 fresh cherries
vanilla ice cream, to serve

PREPARATION TIME
20 minutes

1 Strain all but 2 tbsp of the cherry syrup into a saucepan. Measure the cornstarch into a small bowl with the remaining syrup and combine.

2 Bring the syrup in the saucepan to a boil. Stir in the cornstarch and syrup mixture and simmer briefly to thicken.

3 Add the cherries, stir in the kirsch and spread onto a metal tray to cool.

chocolate

chocolate ice cream

cherries

black cherries

cornstarch

whipping cream
cake

4 Whip the cream with the sugar.

5 Place a spoonful of cherries in the bottom of four sundae glasses. Continue with layers of ice cream, chocolate cake, whipped cream and more cherries until the glasses are full.

COOK'S TIP

Bottled black cherries often have a better flavor than canned, especially if the pits are left in. You needn't remove the pits – just remember to warn your guests.

6 Finish with a piece of chocolate cake, two scoops of ice cream and more whole cream. Decorate with fresh cherries.

Chocolate Chip Banana Crêpes

Serve these delicious crêpes as a dessert topped with cream and toasted almonds.

Makes 16

INGREDIENTS
2 ripe bananas
scant 1 cup milk
2 eggs
1 ¼ cups self-rising flour
⅓ cup ground almonds
1 tbsp superfine sugar
1 oz plain chocolate chips
butter, for frying
pinch of salt

FOR THE TOPPING
⅔ cup heavy cream
1 tbsp confectioners' sugar
½ cup toasted slivered almonds,
    to decorate

PREPARATION TIME

5 minutes

COOKING TIME

15 minutes

chocolate chips

bananas

flour

eggs

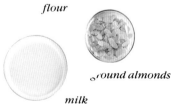
ground almonds
milk

1 In a bowl, mash the bananas with a fork, combine with half of the milk and beat in the eggs. Sieve in the flour, ground almonds, sugar and salt. Make a well in the center and pour in the remaining milk. Add the chocolate chips and stir to produce a thick batter.

2 Heat a knob of butter in a non-stick frying pan. Spoon the crêpe mixture into heaps, allowing room for them to spread. When bubbles emerge, turn the crêpes over and cook briefly on the other side.

3 Loosely whip the cream with the confectioners' sugar to sweeten it slightly. Spoon the cream onto crêpes and decorate with slivered almonds.

COOK'S TIP

For banana and blueberry crêpes, replace the chocolate with 1 cup fresh blueberries. Hot crêpes are also delicious when accompanied by ice cream.

Broiled Pineapple with Rum-custard Sauce

Freshly ground black pepper may seem an unusual ingredient to put with pineapple, until you realise that peppercorns are the fruit of a tropical vine. If the idea does not appeal, make the sauce without pepper.

Serves 4

INGREDIENTS
1 ripe pineapple
2 tbsp butter
fresh strawberries, sliced, to serve

FOR THE SAUCE
1 egg
2 egg yolks
2 tbsp superfine sugar
2 tbsp dark rum
½ tsp freshly ground black pepper

PREPARATION TIME

10 minutes

COOKING TIME

5 minutes

butter

rum

eggs

pineapple

black pepper

superfine sugar

1 Remove the top and bottom from the pineapple with a serrated knife. Fare away the outer skin from top to bottom, remove the core and cut into slices.

2 Preheat a moderate broiler. Dot the pineapple slices with butter and broil for about 5 minutes.

3 To make the sauce, place all the ingredients in a bowl. Set over a saucepan of simmering water and whisk with a hand-held mixer for about 3–4 minutes or until foamy and cooked. Scatter the strawberries over the pineapple and serve with the sauce.

COOK'S TIP

The sweetest pineapples are picked and exported when ripe. Contrary to popular belief, pineapples do not ripen well after picking. Choose fruit that smells sweet and yields to firm pressure from your thumbs.

Apples and Raspberries in Rose Pouchong Syrup

Inspiration for this dessert stems from the fact that the apple and the raspberry belong to the rose family. The subtle flavors are shared here in an infusion of rose-scented tea.

Serves 4

INGREDIENTS
1 tsp rose pouchong tea
1 tsp rose water (optional)
¼ cup sugar
1 tsp lemon juice
5 dessert apples
1½ cups fresh raspberries

PREPARATION TIME

10 minutes

COOKING TIME

5 minutes

tea

apples

sugar

raspberries

COOK'S TIP

If fresh raspberries are out of season, use the same weight of frozen fruit or a 14 oz can of well drained fruit.

1 Warm a large tea pot. Add the rose pouchong tea and 3¾ cups of boiling water together with the rose water, if using. Allow the tea to stand and infuse for 4 minutes.

2 Measure the sugar and lemon juice into a stainless steel saucepan. Strain in the tea and stir to dissolve the sugar.

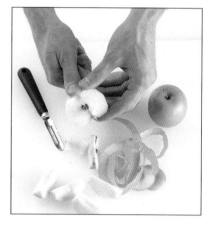

3 Peel and core the apples, then cut into quarters.

4 Poach the apples in the syrup for about 5 minutes.

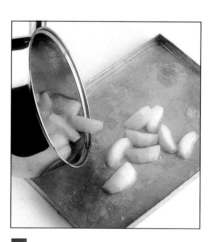

5 Transfer the apples and syrup to a large metal tray and leave to cool to room temperature.

6 Pour the cooled apples and syrup into a bowl, add the raspberries and mix to combine. Spoon into individual glass dishes or bowls and serve warm.

INDEX